Praise for **ANY**

"*Any Insights Yet?* tackles one o
misunderstood concepts in mark
tone. Kocek uses creativity, comr   ....., ...a real world
cases to provide an easy-to-follow blueprint so readers can
learn to ultimately uncover and cultivate their own insights. It's
a wonderful resource for anyone from a senior strategist to an
undergraduate student."

–DAN COHEN, SVP, EXECUTIVE CREATIVE DIRECTOR, SAATCHI NEW YORK

"Insights are intimidating, even for experienced strategists
Any Insights Yet? makes them more approachable both in
terminology and technique - including literal comic inspiration.
Chris not only clearly lays out his points of view without getting
stuck in semantics; he valuably plays out the process, tools, and
tips to building effective insights."

–SETH GAFFNEY, CHIEF STRATEGY OFFICER, PREACHER

"Read this book and you'll enjoy learning what insights are
and what they are not, how to uncover and discover them, and
most importantly, how to put them to work to make meaningful
change. Chris Kocek is a terrific guide and you'll enjoy the
journey. That's a prediction, not an insight."

– MARK DIMASSIMO, CEO, DIMASSIMO GOLDSTEIN

"*Any Insights Yet?* manages to define one of the most
controversial, overused, and misused words in advertising in a
way that removes all the "fuzz" and mysticism and puts it in the
most simple and useful terms. A must-read for anyone looking
for an actionable toolkit for finding and building better insights."

– MARIA PAZOS, GROUP PLANNING DIRECTOR, CARMICHAEL LYNCH

"If developing insights were easy, everyone would be doing it. When it comes to the art of getting to an insight, Chris has clearly articulated the good, the bad, and the helpful at a time when the ever changing landscape of communications needs it most. This book is another great reminder of the power of ideas, the science that goes into the creative process, and most importantly the humanity that can exist in communications. An essential read for anyone interested in developing ideas."

–JUSTIN GRAHAM, GROUP CEO, M&C SAATCHI AUSTRALIA

"Any Insights Yet? is one of the best books I have come across for strategists, brand managers, marketers, or anyone looking for careers in those fields. Kocek is a great storyteller, and he keeps things moving with lots of real-world examples, resulting in great ideas for how to gain true insight about your brand. It's fast, fun, and easy to read."

– ASSAF AVNI, PROFESSOR OF ADVERTISING CREATIVITY, CAL-STATE FULLERTON

"Over the last five years, marketers increasingly believe that consumer insights can be delivered by AI to take advantage of the explosion of data from a myriad of sources. Unfortunately, these attempts have provided mountains of facts but nary an insight. *Any Insights Yet?* is a refreshingly simple and straightforward resource that discerns facts from insights and also provides a useful framework to elucidate insight creation. A must-read for college students and young professionals embarking on any marketing career."

–JOANN SCIARRINO, PROFESSOR OF ADVERTISING, MOODY COLLEGE OF COMMUNICATION, THE UNIVERSITY OF TEXAS AT AUSTIN

Endorsements from industry professionals are the opinions of the cited commentators and do not necessarily reflect the opinions of their agencies or organizations.

ANY

Connect the dots.

INSIGHTS

Create new categories.

YET?

Transform your business.

CHRIS KOCEK

YELLOW BIRD PRESS

Any Insights Yet? is a work of nonfiction. Nonetheless, some names and personal characteristics of individuals or events have been changed in order to disguise identities. Any resulting resemblance to persons living or dead is entirely coincidental and unintentional. Endorsements and advice from industry professionals are the opinions of the cited commentators and do not necessarily reflect the opinions of their agencies or organizations.

Copyright © 2023 by Chris Kocek

All rights reserved.

Published in the United States of America by Yellow Bird Press

ISBN: 978-0-9892849-3-6

Library of Congress Control Number: 2023916896

Illustrations by Cristina Romero and J.D. Mossburg

10 9 8 7 6 5 4 3 2 1

Without limiting the rights under copyright reserved above, no part of this publication may be reproduced, stored in or introduced into a retrieval system, or transmitted, in any form or by any means (electronic, mechanical, photocopying, recording or otherwise), without the prior written permission of the copyright owner above.

The scanning, uploading, and distribution of this book via the Internet or via any other means without the permission of the author is illegal and punishable by law. Please purchase only authorized electronic editions and do not participate in or encourage electronic piracy of copyrighted materials.

*For my kids, Naomi and Leo, whose insights
make the world new again every day.*

CONTENTS

IF YOU SAY THAT WORD ONE MORE TIME...

Sometimes, when I'm in meetings, I like to play a game. I keep track of how many times the word "insight" gets used. One time I was in a meeting that lasted just under 60 minutes and the word was abused 72 times. No kidding.

> → "What's the insight here?"
>
> → "Have we found any insights yet?"
>
> → "Do we have enough insights in our presentation?"
>
> → "Which of these are game-changing insights?"
>
> → "I think we need some bigger insights."
>
> → "Where can we look to get more insights?"
>
> → "Can you get me five more insights by EOD?"

If you're ever in the mood to test your sanity, you should try playing the game yourself. You'll be amazed how often you can reach a new high score.

There have even been times during kickoff meetings, after I've just barely learned the basics about the brand and the challenges they're facing, when the client will casually turn to me and ask, "So...any initial insights?" Of course not. It's not as though I can pull out a magic wand and conjure up some insights with a flick of my wrist. *Expecto insightus!* But I can't say that — the stakes are too high — and I can't bring myself to say the word "insight" one more time. What I really want to do is quote Inigo Montoya from *The Princess Bride*: "You keep using that word. I do not think it means what you think it means." But if I want to keep the client happy, I have to be more diplomatic than that. So usually I'll just say, "Not quite yet, but this is a great start."

It's tough, because somewhere along the way, this word "insight" began to proliferate. Somehow, in conference rooms and investor meetings, we ended up in a "nuclear arms race" of insights.

It's probably because at some point, someone important said they had an insight, and from that point on everyone else felt like they had to have one too.

Lately, I've noticed that the word "insight" has found its way into a number of impressive sounding job titles and department headings. There are teams of people who work in the "Consumer Insights and Analytics" department. At some companies, there's a "Head of Consumer Insights." Sometimes, people even give themselves completely made-up job titles that sound really important, like "Chief Insight Officer."

But if so many people are in charge of insights, how come so many businesses and new product launches fail? If there are so many insights out there, how come there are so many bad creative campaigns? The truth is it's because most people don't know what an insight actually is. That's why I decided to write this book. I hope you find it insightful. *And* useful.

PART 1:

WHAT THE
%#$!
IS AN INSIGHT?

IT'S COMPLICATED

If you type the word "insights" into Google, you'll get back more than three billion results. If you look it up in the dictionary, you'll get one of the following definitions:

in·sight

/'in, sīt/ *noun*
a deep understanding of a person or thing

Merriam Webster:
The power or act of seeing into a situation.
The act or result of apprehending the inner nature of things or of seeing intuitively.

Cambridge Dictionary
A clear, deep, and sometimes sudden understanding of a complicated problem or situation.

If you venture beyond the classic dictionary definitions and ask ten different people what an insight is, chances are you're going to get ten different answers. I know. I speak from experience. I interviewed dozens of people for this book – strategists, copywriters, creative directors, professors, futurists, C-suite executives, artists, priests, rabbis, and more – and I read hundreds of articles that claimed to be chock-full of insights, and here's what I can tell you. The "definitions" are all over the place. I think that's because insights are a little bit like unicorns. They're elusive. They're hard to capture. Even if you think you have one, you may have a hard time describing it. More often than not, when you try to share your insight or your definition of an insight, you end up sounding like someone trying to explain a transcendental experience after being abducted by aliens.

Here's just a small sampling of the kinds of answers people shared with me when I asked them, "How would you define an insight?" While there are some overlaps about truth and understanding and action, you'll see that there's an interesting swirl of dust around the idea of what an insight actually is.

An insight is something that is commonly held to be true. It might have something to do with a spiritual belief, which doesn't withstand the scrutiny of science. It can't just be a statement of truth, though. It has to be something that would make people act or respond.

— Creative Director

It's that thing that everyone wants and is looking for. It's the power of unlocking a subconscious truth. It's a truth that is under a few layers, but you have to dig. It's not just sitting on the surface for anyone to see.

— Advertising Professor

When you mention it — whether it's about a particular brand or the purpose of a company — people say, huh, that is true, I never really thought of it that way before.

— Designer

I don't think an insight is a thing. It's a moment. It's a moment where you have direction. You know what an insight is when it's very human and awesome and people know what to do. It's a rallying point. You know you have it when you see progress happening — when you see people making their own connection and it begins to infect others.

— Chief Strategy Officer & Agency Partner

At its simplest, an insight is something that is seemingly obvious that has tension and can unlock a point of view or way of looking at the world.

— Chief Strategy Officer

I'm not sure if this is an industry cliché, but an insight is that "aha" or "ka-ching" moment. An insight needs to be something that looks deeper into motivations and behavior. It's a penetrating understanding that goes beyond observation about why people do what they do that can then be commercialized.

— Brand Strategist

An insight is a product of an exercise. It's a process of making connections. It's not just finding the truth itself. There is also an element of articulation — that's the role of the planner in the process. Finding an insight by itself is like finding a diamond. You don't find insights. Maybe you build them? It's like making a map. You develop them. You articulate them. You make the connections that bring them to life.

— Chief Strategy Officer

Insights have to be within the right context and have to be relevant to the issue or topic at hand. An insight is something that changes the way someone looks at something, leading them to take a different action than they're doing today.

— CEO of Large SEO Firm

An insight is something that disrupts conventional wisdom. It's not something that's well known. It has to be something that's true and observable and measurable, but until now it hasn't really been recognized.

— Brand Strategy Director

It's the most bantered around word in our industry, but at the same time it's the most misunderstood as well. There's an analytical layer and a strategic layer. That's still the art vs. the science of coming up with insights. With big data, you can do a bunch of modeling, testing, and number crunching, which can start to tell a story, but usually there's a gap between the data and the insight. The bridge is understanding the "why." Why are people doing what they're doing?

— Chief Strategy Officer & Agency Partner

An insight is informed intuition. It's the ability to take in a lot of information and put the right filters on so that you can see things more clearly. It's about perspective. If I'm able to see something of relevance or value that may not be obvious to everyone else, that's when I think I have an insight.

— Futurist

An insight is a unique understanding of human nature and human truth as to why we behave and act the way that we do. It's unique and unconventional and usually there's some kind of tension.

— Brand Strategist

An insight needs to be innately human. The best insights are universal while at the same time being deeply personal. An insight should be a little surprising and it should have a little tension in it. A tension between what an individual wants and isn't necessarily getting or seeing. Insights are usually hidden in plain sight.

— **Chief Strategy Officer**

To me, it comes down to being a nugget of truth that you're able to act on or inspire someone or create upon. Most of the time, it's something that requires some understanding of a particular customer group or situation. The purpose of it is to inspire some action or creativity.

— **Brand Strategist**

An insight is seeing something in a way you never really thought about before that's grounded in a human truth.

— **Chief Creative Officer**

✷ ✷ ✷

Great. That's about as much consensus as you'd find at a climate change summit at the United Nations. Let's try this a different way. Let's start with what an insight definitely is NOT.

AN INSIGHT IS NOT AN OBSERVATION

Most of the time, when people use the word insight, what they really mean is observation. They came. They saw. They called their observation an insight. Let's look at a few examples:

→ Athletes get into the zone by listening to music before the game begins.

→ People use Pinterest to get inspiration for birthday parties, weddings, home décor, and more.

→ Parents often feel time-poor and wish they had an easier way to make their kids' lunches.

→ Buying a mattress is an awkward consumer experience.

While most of these observations fall into the "no duh" category, that doesn't mean they're useless. In fact, some of them have led to important innovations and award-winning campaigns. But anybody could go to a sporting event and see athletes wearing headphones before the game. You could spend time with a multi-tasking mom for five minutes and see she's got a lot on her plate. If you've ever bought a mattress before, you know it's a strange experience at best — lying down on a dozen unmade beds, trying to simulate various sleeping positions while wondering how many other people have been on those same beds earlier in the day.

The good news about observations: everyone has the ability to pay attention to the world around them, and observations are a great place to start the process of building insights. The not-so-good news: you're going to need more than just one or two observations to get to an insight.

COMIC "INSIGHTS"

Comedians are often said to be insightful. And some of them really are. Over the course of a single set, or even just a few minutes, they'll connect the dots between observations in a way that is truly eye-opening. But most of the time their "insights" are really just extremely keen observations. They notice behaviors that most people don't pay attention to, and they have an elegant, disarming way of pointing out the taboos and embarrassing things we do on a daily basis, but which we never really talk about. As the old saying goes, it's funny because it's true.

Underneath the specifics, though, many comedians who do observational humor are really saying the same thing and asking the same question.

Comedian:

Do you ever notice this weird thing that people do?
That we all do?

Audience:

[Laughing]. Yes. Oh my gosh, yes. I've done that.

Comedian:

Isn't it ridiculous that we do that?

Audience:

[Laughing while wiping away the tears.] Yes. It's true.
It's ridiculous. I'm ridiculous. We're all so ridiculous.
You're hilarious.

Comedian:

Why do we do that?

(Note: the comedian may not come right out and ask
that question, but the question is always implied.)

Why do we leave a few drops of milk in the milk carton and put it back in the fridge instead of just throwing the carton away? Why do we stare at people who cut us off in traffic as though we're trying to memorize their features for a sketch artist at the police station? When we forget someone's name, why do we avoid them instead of just asking them to remind us of their name?

The ability to ask these questions — Why do we do these things? Why do we behave this way? Why do we accept all of these norms that society has created for us? — can sometimes make comedians seem far more profound than politicians or priests.

But before you go hiring a bunch of comedians to run your Consumer Insights Department, you have to understand that most of the time comedians don't actually ANSWER the clever questions they ask. First, they make an interesting observation or they highlight an amusing tension, then they diffuse that tension with a punchline (or two or three or four), and then, once they've run out of punchlines, they move on to another interesting observation.

Even though their observations are keen and pithy and true (three characteristics that every insight must have), it's hard to connect the dots between their observations and the complex business problem that you're trying to solve. Comedians have an amazing power to tell the unvarnished truth to our faces, but one of the reasons their observations rarely rise to the level of insight is because they don't persuade you to change your behavior.

At the end of the day, the job of the comedian is to hold a mirror up to society and make us reflect on ourselves, but comedians rarely try to answer the question, "Why do we do these things?" As a planner, strategist or the VP of Consumer Insights, that's your job.

THE POWER OF OBSERVATION

Here's the thing — an insight is not *always* a prerequisite for a successful brand campaign. Sometimes a great observation by itself *can* inspire a game-changing idea. Just look at Snickers and their famous campaign, "You're Not You When You're Hungry."

Like any good comedian, someone on the Snickers marketing team probably noticed two co-workers yelling at each other for no apparent reason right around lunch time. The "marketing genius" who observed that behavior pointed it out during a meeting, and from then on everyone started seeing it on a grand scale (aka the universal human truth), and as a team, they came up with a campaign thought-starter: "You're not really yourself when you're hungry. You become someone else, like something out of *Dr. Jekyll and Mr. Hyde*. You go a little crazy. You act like a jerk. You say stupid things. In short, you're hangry."

And just like at a comedy show, everyone at the briefing table probably laughed and said, "Yes! Oh my gosh, yes! It's so true. It's ridiculous, but it's true. I can be such a jerk when I get hangry!"

And then Snickers solved all of our problems in the world by saying (and I'm paraphrasing), "Don't worry. Next time you're feeling hangry, just eat a Snickers. Because Snickers really satisfies." You know, because of peanuts.

Amazing, right? I mean, seriously, it's a candy bar. It's a chocolate covered candy bar with nougat, caramel, twenty grams of sugar, and maybe ten peanuts per bar. But what a campaign! What an amazing, acrobatic twist from, "You're hangry" to "Now go eat a Snickers!" And sure, ANY snack brand could have made this same observation — you're not you when you're hungry — but not all snack brands could pull it off like Snickers. A brand of kale chips could never legitimately say, "Kale chips can really satisfy the angry beast inside of you when you're hangry." Nobody would believe it.

So keep that in mind the next time you're trying to connect the dots between an amusing observation and your brand. There has to be something believable about your brand as the payoff to that pain point. Otherwise, *your brand* will end up becoming the punchline.

AN INSIGHT
IS NOT A
DATA POINT

In the era of big data, it's popular to use data points as synonyms for insights. In article after article and case study after award-winning case study, people will highlight an interesting statistic and call it an insight. It's one of the main reasons the word insight has proliferated. Data is everywhere, so insights must be everywhere. Right? **Wrong.**

Here are just a few examples from online articles that say, "The Insight" when they should have just said, "The data."

*The **Insight Data:*** a study conducted by XYZ company revealed that 80% of women in the US aged between 25-55 agree that they are their own worst critic.

*The **Insight Data:*** At puberty, 49% of girls feel paralyzed by a fear of failure, leading them to avoid trying new things.

*The **Insight Data:*** 60% of women buy body wash for their men.

*The **Insight Data:*** 81% of people who use dating apps have never found a long-term relationship on any swiping app.

*The **Insight Data:*** 24% of Americans ages 35-44 would prefer to get a root canal than negotiate with a car dealer.

*The **Insight Data:*** Today, more households have single people than married people.

*The **Insight Data:*** 62% of nursing moms say they have nursed their baby or pumped milk in a bathroom stall.

Don't get me wrong. I'm not trying to say data isn't important. These are all powerful data points, and many of them have been used as springboards for highly engaging, multi-million-dollar ad campaigns, but data is not the same thing as an insight. Anyone could conduct a survey and ask similar questions or subscribe to a service like Mintel that aggregates dozens of surveys and get access to similar data. It's what you *do* with the data that makes a difference.

Case in point: P&G (and Old Spice) had known for years from various surveys that women were responsible for making more than half of all body wash purchases. But P&G had never really done anything with that data from a creative or media planning standpoint. That is, until they launched their award-winning campaign "The Man Your Man Could Smell Like," which targeted men and women for the very first time, with the goal of getting couples to have a bigger conversation about body wash. Compared to previous efforts, this new campaign took a novel approach to media planning as well, targeting couples at movie theaters and other situations around Valentine's Day, to create that spark of conversation that could potentially lead to behavior change and new purchasing habits (in favor of Old Spice, of course).

Was the Old Spice campaign built on an insight? I don't mean to offend anyone here, but I don't think so. I think they leveraged existing data and used it as a springboard to make a brilliant campaign that created buzz and increased sales. No insight required. At the end of the day, data points are often a key component to building an insight, but raw data by itself isn't enough, even if you have lots of it. It's a little bit like raw ingredients thrown into a pan – it's not really a meal at that point. But take those raw ingredients, add some cooking oil, a little heat, some seasoning, a little bit of time, and a dash of imagination, and maybe it'll congeal into a secret sauce that you can legitimately call an insight.

COMEDIAN SPOTLIGHT: A DATA-DRIVEN JOKE

"I saw a study that said speaking in front of a crowd is considered the number one fear of the average person. Number two was death. This means to the average person, if you have to be at a funeral, you would rather be in the casket than doing the eulogy."

—Jerry Seinfeld

AN INSIGHT IS NOT A BASIC HUMAN TRUTH

There are a lot of basic human truths out there, but most of them aren't very useful in a business context. You know the kind I'm talking about - the obvious truths that are borderline cliches: "It is what it is. Wherever you go, there you are. Life is short, so make the most of it." These may all be true, but they're kind of like pieces of art hanging in a hotel conference room. They're just kind of there for ambience, but they have no stopping power. They don't fill you with any real emotion. If you do notice them, you might just say, "That's nice," and move on.

MORE BASIC HUMAN TRUTHS

I don't think anyone would disagree with any of these truths, but just because something is true doesn't mean it's an insight. As the dictionary says, "an insight is a deep understanding of a person or thing," but these truths don't go very deep. So the question is, if we're looking for real insights, how do we push these truths into new territories to reveal something deeper?

I promise we'll get to that later. For now, though, just remember, you don't always need an insight to make a great campaign or a new product or service innovation. A basic human truth combined with the right creative idea can move the needle for your business or lead you to an entirely new business model, putting your brand at the forefront of the cultural conversation.

FROM TRUTH TO INNOVATION

Basic human truth: People get angry when they're hungry.
Snickers campaign: You're not you when you're hungry. Snickers really satisfies.

Basic human truth: People get bored doing the same workout.
New business models and ideas: Class Pass. Camp Gladiator. Orange Theory. Countless fitness apps.

Basic human truth: People aren't confident when it comes to choosing their personal fashion.
New business models: Stitch Fix, Trunk Club, Wantable, etc.

Here's another basic human truth that everyone has experienced at one time or another. People are afraid to try new things. I've seen this behavior time and again with myself, family, and friends. As spontaneous as we all think we are, the truth is most of us are afraid of risk. It's one of the oldest truths out there, and it doesn't matter what category you're in. That's why Costco offers free samples. That's why software companies offer free trials. That's why car dealerships let you drive before you buy. This truth — this fear of risk — is a major problem for most brands, because when you have customers who only get one or two items from you, you're in a danger zone. That's why you have to keep innovating.

Restaurants, in particular, have to deal with people's fear of risk, and the way most of them handle this issue is by offering some kind of "satisfaction guarantee." If you don't like something, we'll replace it. Simple enough, right? But here's a different approach (and campaign headline) for restaurants trying to overcome this basic human truth of risk aversion: **Try It Free Tuesdays.** Here's how it works. Come in on a Tuesday evening (a traditionally slow day for most restaurants) and order your favorite main entree as usual. Then, if you're interested, you can have a side portion of another main dish (which we'll be batch creating at scale) for free.

For the customer, the upside is obvious — they get to try something new every Tuesday, risk-free. But for the restaurant there are several business driving benefits. In addition to getting more traffic to your restaurant, you'll be giving your customers more reasons to love you, which means more reasons to come back more often. This idea isn't rocket science. It's like "kids eat free" but with a different set of goals.

The bottom line: you don't always need an insight to make an impact to your business. Sometimes, if you just combine a basic human truth with a tried-and-true marketing tactic and give it a different name, you can drive traffic and increase sales. The only catch is if the tactic works, everyone else will do it, too. That's the problem with tactics. They're easy to copy.

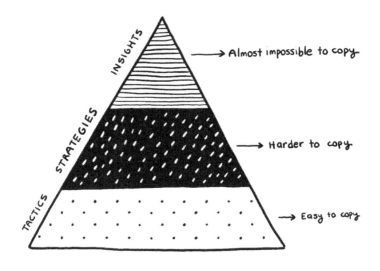

TRUTH IS A LOT LIKE GLASS.
YOU CAN HEAT IT UP AND
STRETCH IT AND TWIST IT AND
BEND IT IN DIFFERENT WAYS. IN
THE RIGHT HANDS AND IN THE
RIGHT LIGHT, IT CAN BECOME
AN INSIGHT, REVEALING AND
REFRACTING MULTIPLE TRUTHS
THAT YOU NEVER NOTICED
BEFORE. BUT AN INSIGHT, LIKE
GLASS, IS DELICATE. MORE
OFTEN THAN NOT, IT SHATTERS
DURING THE PROCESS. DON'T
GIVE UP, THOUGH. JUST SWEEP
UP ALL THE BROKEN PIECES,
PUT THEM BACK IN THE FIRE,
AND TRY AGAIN.

AN INSIGHT
IS <u>NOT</u>
A TREND

A lot of researchers will use the word insights when they're talking about trends. Shame on them. They should know better. Trends are just a collection of data points wrapped up in pithy one liners. Here are some examples:

The ~~Insight~~ Trend: More Millennials are going vegan.

The ~~Insight~~ Trend: Young people are buying fewer cars today compared to ten years ago.

The Insight Trend: Portable snack options are increasingly important for on-the-go consumers.

The Insight Trend: More consumers are using virtual assistants to help with everyday tasks.

The Insight Trend: Trust in societal institutions is waning.

All of these trends are true. And a good trend report should have multiple sources of data to support them. But the reason a trend is not the same thing as an insight is because it doesn't go to the trouble of explaining WHY these things are happening.

To get to the why, you have to take a step back and look at different trends in the aggregate. You have to do what I like to call "The Beautiful Mind" trick, based on the film *A Beautiful Mind* with Russell Crowe. You have to take a combination of trends – they can be adjacent trends or opposing trends – line them up on a whiteboard and ask yourself (or the rest of your team) why these things are happening at the same time. What's the pattern behind the trends, what's the potential tension, and what's the bigger, tectonic shift that they're creating in our society?

And then perhaps, most importantly for your business, you have to ask yourself how you can leverage that tectonic shift to change your product design, your delivery system, or your messaging.

That's exactly what MasterCard did with their "Priceless" campaign. They identified an emerging trend that indicated an important shift in society's definition of success. A combination of surveys and actual spending data helped them identify the trend, highlighting how people were less interested in acquiring more stuff (aka material success) and were becoming more interested in "collecting" more meaningful experiences (aka intangible markers of success). Thus, the "Priceless" campaign was born, with MasterCard focusing on specific situations and experiences – the feeling that some things are worth so much, they're priceless. Of course, that warm and fuzzy feeling only lasts until you get your next credit card statement, but who cares? It's the experience right now that counts!

What's interesting is how this trend – the changing definition of success and the desire to have more meaningful experiences –

when combined with a whole host of other societal, economic, and technology trends (e.g. people waiting longer to get married, people never learning how to cook, and the ability of companies to use big data to create mass customization) is the reason for the rise of new business models like Blue Apron and Hello Fresh.

Again, to be clear, a single trend is not an insight. But if you're able to combine different trends and see a pattern underneath those trends that no one else can see (aka a deep understanding), then you might be on the verge of an insight. Then again, just like in the movie *A Beautiful Mind* you might also be imagining patterns that aren't really there.

AN INSIGHT IS <u>NOT</u> A TAGLINE, A JINGLE, A SLOGAN, OR A CATCHPHRASE

I have no doubt that the "The Most Interesting Man in The World" from Dos Equis is full of insights, but that line in and of itself, is NOT an insight.

One of the hallmarks of an insight is how simple and concise it is, which may very well be why so many people mischaracterize a catchphrase or a tagline as being "insightful." But a catchphrase is just a clever bit of copy. It can often be taken straight out of a focus group transcription and polished into something with a little more alliteration. I'm not saying it's easy, but let's call a catch-phrase a catchphrase and not confuse it with an insight.

There are a lot of brands that have been built or revived over the years thanks to great slogans or catchphrases or taglines, but the problem with these clever turns of phrase is that they can feel dated over time or they can self-immolate if they get used too often. Here are a few examples.

Wassssuuuuuuuuuuup?
(Budweiser)

Can you hear me now?
(Verizon)

Got Milk?
(Milk)

What's in your wallet?
(Capital One)

The Best a Man Can Get.
(Gillette)

It keeps going...and going...and going.
(Energizer)

I'm not saying an insight, like a diamond, is forever. (See what I just did there?) Insights, like taglines, can be just as much a product of the times they come from, and if the cultural sands have shifted since you had your big brand-building insight five or ten years ago, then that may be why your brand is no longer as relevant or has gotten buried by the competition.

Taglines and catchphrases can be a great distillation of what your brand is about, and if they're written well enough or paired with the right music (Sing it with me now: "What would you do-ooh-ooh for a Klondike Bar?") they can help your business stay top of mind, which is incredibly valuable.

That said, if I had to choose between a tagline and an insight, I'd put my money on the insight.

AN INSIGHT
IS <u>NOT</u>
AN IDEA

This one's a bit of a paradox, so let me explain. Ideas can be incredibly powerful. But ideas are also cheap. They don't cost anything to produce (other than the time to come up with them and write them down), and if you go into a brainstorm session with a bunch of colleagues, you can probably fill up an entire whiteboard with hundreds of ideas in less than an hour. At the end of the session, you can have a good laugh at some of the over-the-top ideas and use colorful stickers to identify which ideas are most promising. But those kinds of ideas, while plentiful, are probably not insights. That's because most brainstorms are trying to answer a simple question with a tactical answer.

→ WHAT SHOULD WE NAME
OUR NEW PRODUCT OFFERING?

→ WHERE ELSE CAN WE CONNECT
WITH OUR TARGET AUDIENCE?

→ HOW CAN WE INCREASE TRAFFIC
AND GENERATE MORE SALES?

That last one is probably the most commonly asked question in conference rooms across the planet. And if you ask me, it might even be an insight *killer*. That's because it's too broad, it's starting from the wrong place, and it's pointing people in the wrong direction. Everyone wants to know how to generate more sales, but when you ask people to come up with ideas for doing that, more often than not, they'll come up with gimmicks – quick, tactical ideas that will generate short term gains.

But those short term gains won't redefine the category or transform you into a category leader. If the idea is simple (and most sales generating ideas are), someone else will inevitably copy it and then you're back to square one, neck and neck with your competitors, instead of being light years ahead.

PROVEN IDEAS TO INCREASE TRAFFIC AND GENERATE MORE SALES

No matter how much you want to work on mind-blowing, game-changing, category-disrupting insights, there will always be pressure from the marketing and sales departments to increase sales quickly. The following are some tried and true tactical ideas that work across multiple categories. Keep these in your back pocket for your next brainstorm session so that you can save your brainpower for your next big insight.

- Create a low-price, entry-level option or low-price combo deal. For fast food and quick service restaurants, it's the $1 menu board or the "5 meals under $5" menu. What's your version of this in *your* category?

- Offer bounce back cash or variable discounts if the customer comes back again within a short period of time. It goes something like this: You just bought something from us. Come back in the next week or the next few hours and buy something else and we'll give you X% off. Starbucks, Kohl's, VistaPrint, and countless others do this all the time.

- Create a rewards program. Anything from a paper punch card to a mobile app. Not only will you learn more about your target audience's shopping habits, but you can test different incentives to see which ones work best for higher dollar spend and greater frequency.

- Try before you buy. This works for software (aka the freemium model), new cars, and countless food products. When combined with the right data and carefully calculated shipping logistics, this tactic has become a business model unto itself, with countless snack boxes acting as an aggregated sampling box for different brands. I'm amazed that brands like Unilever or Mondelez haven't come up with their own sampler subscription boxes for introducing new brands to their loyal fans.

- Make it an "invitation only" offer with a reward for both parties. Banks use this incentive all the time for opening a new checking account – both parties get $25. Facebook did a version of this when they first launched. "Membership" was only available to people in college. Google did this when launching Gmail. Most online businesses these days offer a version of this "invitation only" approach as it creates a feeling of exclusivity.

- Offer friends and family "flash" sales. This is like a cousin to the "invitation only" offer. Almost every online store has done this at some point or another.

- Run a contest or a giveaway (said every social media marketing manager ever).

- Donate a portion of the proceeds to your favorite charity or your customers' favorite cause. (Instead of doing this once a month or once a quarter, some businesses like Tom's, Bombas, and Warby Parker have built this idea into their business model.)

- Trade in _____ for a discount on _____. Trade in your old phone from X brand for a new phone from the competitive brand. Trade in a worn-out pair of jeans from X brand for a new pair from Y brand. Not only can you get people to give you a try with this kind of incentive, but you'll also be getting a lot of valuable competitive data since you'll discover which brands people are most willing to trade in to get yours.

It's important to note that every single one of the ideas just mentioned was a great idea for the company that implemented it first. But it didn't take long before everyone else in the category copied the idea and took away that competitive advantage. That's why I say ideas can be cheap. If they're easily copied, they're not as valuable in the long run.

Sometimes, though, you can make people think an idea is an insight with a simple trick. Change the context or the category of the original idea and layer it onto something new.

That's exactly what JetBlue did back in the day with their "All You Can Jet" campaign – unlimited flights within a 30-day period (to be used between September and October; traditionally a slow travel period) for a shockingly low price of $499 or $699.

Was this idea an insight? No. It was an idea taken out of its normal context. It was an "all you can eat" restaurant idea (flat fee pricing) combined with a "happy hour" concept mapped onto a different time frame (one month instead of a few hours). It's brilliant, but it's not an insight.

I'm sure JetBlue had to dig into the data and do some calculations (e.g. how many people will likely take full advantage of this offer, and how much will that cost us?), but at the end of the day, look at how much great PR mileage they got out of this idea. Look at how much additional reach and how many impressions they got for their brand. When this campaign launched, how many people went to the JetBlue website to learn more about it, didn't actually get the "All You Can Jet" pass, but booked a flight or two anyway? Based on the number of years JetBlue has offered this deal, I would wager that they have gotten a very good return on their investment with this idea masquerading as an insight — this idea out of context.

Starbucks has done the same thing with their own happy hour program. Again, restaurants have been doing happy hours for years. But a coffee shop running a happy hour? Now that's revolutionary! The genius behind most of Starbucks' marketing initiatives is the way they layer their ideas to maximize their data, which they then leverage to maximize their sales. First, you have to get the Starbucks app to activate the happy hour deal. The app is a big data gateway that let's Starbucks learn more about you than you probably know about yourself — what you buy, which days and *times of day* you buy, and which locations you go to most often. The more data they have, the more they can customize the deals to your lifestyle so that you'll keep coming back for more. No insights necessary.

* * *

Again, I'm not trying to downplay the power of a big, new idea. There's no doubt that big ideas can lead to attention-getting campaigns and through-the-roof sales for a lot of major brands. But even simple ideas can create huge gains in terms of sales and short-term competitive advantage. However, these kinds of ideas are still tied to incrementalism. They're usually not category-disrupting, competition-obliterating game-changers. Why? Because they're not insights.

To be fair, an insight *is* technically an idea, but most ideas are shallow. **An insight has roots that go deep.**

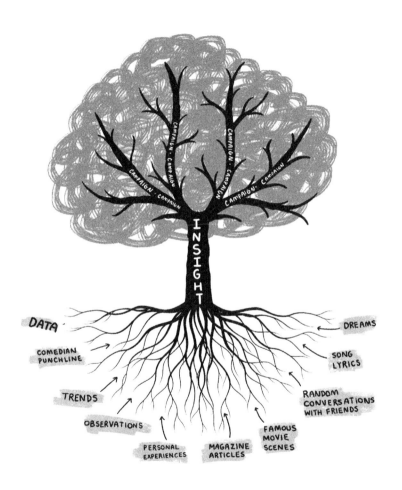

So I hope we can all agree now what an insight is NOT. It's not a single thing. It's not a catchphrase. It's not a single data point. It's not a trend. It's not an observation. An insight is more complex than that. It's a combination of things. And even though it may be something that's hidden in plain sight, it's not exactly something that you *find*. I believe a true insight is something that you *build*.

So without further ado, here is my definition of what an insight actually is – at least within the context of business, branding, and marketing campaigns. (If you're looking for spiritual insights, you've picked up the wrong book.) From here on out, I hope this definition will be adopted as the de facto definition that is used throughout the universe, in perpetuity, for all eternity, unless or until someone comes up with something better.

Ready? Here we go:

An insight is a constellation of data points, observations, and human truths, coming together to solve a particular problem and inspire a new product design, business model, or innovative marketing campaign that gives your brand a long-term competitive advantage.

So there it is. That's my definition wrapped up in a metaphor. An insight is a constellation. But just like any constellation in the night sky, some people may not be able to see your insight right away. Does that mean you don't have an insight? No. It just means you're going to have to help them connect the dots.

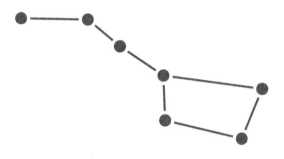

The seven stars clustered around the North Star in the night sky are not inherently "The Big Dipper."

We recognize them as "The Big Dipper" because someone pointed them out to us. The same goes for insights.

KEY CHARACTERISTICS OF AN INSIGHT

While I hate to boil it down to a simple checklist of characteristics, and while I'm sure there's an angry army of consultants, strategists, and marketing practitioners out there who will criticize me for this, I've discovered through countless brainstorms and workshops that this checklist helps people stress test their ideas to see if what they have is an actual insight. The checklist is helpful because many times, on the surface, an idea and an insight can look similar. You might think you have an insight because, "If it walks like a duck and it quacks like a duck, then it probably is a duck." But ducks are a dime a dozen, and what you want is something more unique than that. What you really want is a platypus.

10 CHARACTERISTICS OF A TRUE INSIGHT

→ Clear and concise

→ Contains a universal human truth (or two)

→ Reveals or reframes the "why" behind that truth

→ Surprising, unconventional, or unexpected

→ Taps into a cultural tension

→ Backed by data, observations, or trends

→ Inspires the rest of your team and/or your end consumers

→ Connects back to the problem you're trying to solve or connects to the brand's core attributes

→ Leads to a meaningful action (e.g. a new product, service, business model, or behavior change)

→ Gives your brand a clear advantage over the competition for a meaningful duration of time

If 10 is too many, here's an acronym that can help you.

I nspires action (enough said)

N ot obvious (reframes the problem in a unique way)

S imple to explain (clear and concise language)

I ncludes key data, observations, or trends

G ives your brand a clear advantage (must connect back to the brand)

H uman truth (must be connected to something that every human can relate to)

T aps into a cultural tension (not always, but definitely helps)

If you can honestly check 70% or more of the boxes on either of those lists, then go ahead and pop the cork on that champagne bottle, because you probably have an actual insight. Congratulations! I know that's a lot of boxes to check, but maybe that's why true insights are so rare. As a Chief Strategy Officer once told me, "It's not like I have a shelf of 43 insights out there – I probably haven't had more than five in my entire career."

That's because finding the data, connecting the dots, revealing or reframing the why, stress testing your insight, and then articulating that insight so that others can see it (and be inspired by it) is hard work. It's not something that happens overnight. It takes time to distill all those observations and trends and data points that you've been collecting over the past several weeks (or months) and boil them all down to just one or two sentences. That's the difference between gathering data and building an insight. More often than not, when you start writing it all down, you'll have a bunch of loosely connected thoughts that resemble the ramblings of a madman. You'll have a multi-page manifesto of ideas and observations when what you're *trying* to create is a 17-syllable haiku. Each word of your insight must be carefully chosen, with intention and precision. It's not easy. In fact, it reminds me of that famous quote:

"IF I'D HAD MORE TIME, I WOULD HAVE WRITTEN A SHORTER ~~LETTER~~ INSIGHT."

PART 2:

HOW DO YOU BUILD AN INSIGHT?

FIND THE PATTERNS

The problem with constellations is that they aren't real. They're products of our imagination. They're patterns in the sky that our ancestors built that we have adopted, and they give us a sense of order and direction in an otherwise chaotic universe. I'm sure there were plenty of disagreements among our ancestors about various constellations as well.

How our ancestors saw bears, eagles, or mythical whales in the stars is something of a mystery. But that's why insights are similar to constellations. Most of the time, they require a little bit of explanation and imagination.

I believe that an insight, like a constellation, is something that you build. It's a pattern that you alone can see, at first, and you build it out by connecting the dots between observations, data points, human truths, your own history, personal identity, and a variety of other factors that makes you unique.

In other words, everyone builds insights a little differently. Two people can look at the same data, but because of their personal histories and biases (and sometimes even their neuroses), they won't see the same thing. They may both see a pattern, but they'll draw different conclusions. That's why insights can be so elusive and cause so much controversy. Building insights is one thing. Building consensus among your peers is something else.

Chances are, any time you declare you have an insight, there will be an army of consultants, strategists, and creative directors who will scoff and say, "That's not really an insight." If you think you're onto something though, then you should ask your peers to try to build on it rather than tear it down. Recruit them to find more data dots and human truths so that your insight – your constellation –

can become more instantly recognizable by more people and lead to innovations that will make the world a better place.

On the following pages is an example of an insight I have built based on countless weekends working on various home improvement projects. To illustrate my particular process, I have identified nine key observations (which include macro trends, basic human truths, category truths, and a business-to-consumer tension). From there, I have distilled all of those observations down into what I believe is a pithy insight statement. Then I take that insight and transform it into an actionable, business building idea, highlighting how that business idea, born from the insight, can simultaneously solve all nine key problems/observations.

Now you may disagree with my observations, the insight, or the ultimate business idea, but my intention here is to show you my process. If you like my technique, you're welcome to use it for yourself, your business, or your brand.

Ready? Let's do this.

People don't know how to talk about their DIY projects.

Most people are *not* home improvement experts. When we're trying to fix our leaky faucets or our hissing toilets, we don't usually know the names of the different pieces that need to be replaced, so we go to the home improvement store and we say, "My toilet is hissing. I think I need this thingamabobber to fix it." And unless you bring that thingamabobber with you or you bring a picture of it, the associate (bless them, those patient souls), must act as a translator and try to decipher your gibberish into something more coherent. Sometimes, it can even take an entire team of associates to reverse-engineer the idea of a whatchamacallit into an actual product that can be found on the shelves.

OBSERVATION #2: (building on observation #1)

Things get lost in translation.

So the heroic home improvement associate listens carefully to your garbled description of whatever it is you're working on and says, "OK. This is what you need." And he/she gives you the item that they think you came in for based on your description, but chances are, because you're not a plumber or a home improvement expert, your description was incomplete. You forgot to mention that you have a small bathroom and that your toilet is right next to the bathtub or right next to the sink and that, in order to get access to that thing next to the other thing that needs to be fixed, you're going to need a special kind of wrench or a particular kind of part, or you're going to need to take off some of the tiles on the wall and expose some piping. Which leads to the next problem...

OBSERVATION #3:
Project creep.

What started out as a simple project – a hissing toilet – something that you thought was going to take a couple of hours to fix, ends up taking the entire weekend, or several weekends, because you have to keep going back to the home improvement store because of problems with #1 & #2 (no pun intended).

And, of course, the home improvement store spends tons of money on employee training on a national scale to help their associates talk you through these problems, so that they can help you solve these issues a little faster, but there's only so much these training sessions can do, especially when there are a dozen different toilet types, even more toilet parts, and even more tools that could be used to get the job done.

Meanwhile, the people running the home improvement store probably have data that indicates that every time you come back to the store, you buy other things – impulse purchases or other home-related items (e.g. light bulbs, a roll of duct tape, some plants, etc.) – and that purchase data makes them think, "You know what? Project creep really isn't a bad thing because it benefits our bottom line."

But here's the catch. If you're the consumer, you see things from a totally different angle. You *hate* project creep. Every time you have to go back to the store, you kick yourself for not describing the situation more accurately or for not having the words to describe the full context of the problem (observation #1) and you hate the store just a little more because the associates didn't think to ask you the right questions (part of observation #2) so that you could get all the right parts the first time. At the end of the day, you leave the store with a bad taste in your mouth.

Most people don't want to do these kinds of DIY projects. They just want to enjoy their homes.

The reality is most people don't want to go to the store so often that they know the associates on a first name basis. They don't want to spend all that extra time (and money on gas) going to and from the store. They're not interested in spending their weekend taking a crash course on plumbing via YouTube, watching various videos that may or may not be able to help them solve their problem. They just want the project to be done.

Unless you're a plumber who does this kind of thing for a living, or you're a jovial masochist who loves to spend countless hours second guessing yourself, you don't really want to spend your weekends this way. You want to spend your free time playing with your kids, watching a football game, or relaxing in a hammock.

People don't like walking around large warehouses looking for associates who may not be very knowledgeable about a particular project.

Home improvement stores are really just giant warehouses where the products outnumber the people by a ratio of 3,000 to 1. At any given moment, there are about 20-30 associates on the floor of these 100,000 square-foot behemoths, and those associates' primary job is to stock and organize more than 40,000 different SKUs, so there's no way they can all be experts on every product in the store and every project that comes through the door.

One of the most common complaints about home improvement stores is that A) you can never find someone to help you and B) when you do find someone, they're either too young or too inexperienced to give you the help you need. If you look at customer reviews or home improvement forums, you'll find plenty of comments by customers who were frustrated because they felt they knew more than the associate who was trying to help them.

People are often afraid to get started on home improvement projects.

Projects like remodeling a bathroom, updating a kitchen, or building, sanding, and treating a backyard patio are daunting. People may love the ideation phase – looking at pictures on Pinterest and daydreaming about what their new bathroom, kitchen, or patio will look like – but at some point, inspiration collides with reality. When they go to measure their space, they realize there's an unexpected electrical outlet or an awkwardly shaped pipe, and they don't end up taking those next steps from inspiration to action. They're afraid to get started because:

A) There are so many things they don't know that they're not sure where to begin (aka being overwhelmed).

OR

B) They've had such bad experiences in the past (e.g. simple projects taking a long time) that they end up convincing themselves it will take forever to get this bigger project done, which means they don't do anything at all.

People come to the store with pictures of their projects on their phones.

With just about everyone these days having a smart phone on them at all times, more and more people are coming to their favorite home improvement store with pictures of their projects on their phones, but the fact that people are bringing pictures on their phones in the first place means there's a bridge that's missing. After all, you don't have to bring your phone into Walgreens or CVS to get your photos printed. You can just submit your photos online and pick up prints an hour later.

OBSERVATION #8:

Lost opportunities for the business.

Stores like Home Depot and Lowe's spend a fortune on consumer research (e.g. focus groups, online surveys, in-store intercepts, etc.) to better understand customer wants and needs. The vast majority of conversations at the store level are never captured in a database and so the learnings and opportunities associated with those conversations are lost.

Business-to-consumer tension.

The home improvement store thinks they're in the job of selling products. But the consumer comes into the store looking for products *and* expertise. That's why they walk around looking for an associate. They often want advice as much as they want the products. That's why there are so many "how-to" videos on YouTube. More often than not, the customized expertise is what's missing from the equation, and that tension bubbles up in the form of complaints on home improvement forums all the time. Whenever there's a tension like this, there's bound to be an insight and a much bigger business opportunity.

THE INSIGHT:

IF IT TAKES A THOUSAND WORDS TO DESCRIBE YOUR HOME IMPROVEMENT PROJECT, AND IF A PICTURE IS WORTH A THOUSAND WORDS, THEN WHY NOT START EVERY PROJECT WITH A PICTURE?

Bam. There it is. There's the multi-million-dollar opportunity hiding in plain sight. Can you see it? Can you see all the ways this insight can bring order to the chaos of the home improvement universe, solving all those aforementioned observations while completely transforming the home improvement category?

Not yet? OK. Let's keep going.

FROM INSIGHT TO IDEA TO ACTION

The Insight & The Idea(s):

The insight in this case weaves together multiple issues at the same time, so there's actually more than one idea in here. If pictures are worth a thousand words and if almost everyone has a smart phone with a camera these days, then let's:

1) Build an online portal for people to upload their project pictures (and videos) and their home improvement questions.

2) Build a network of online experts to answer those questions.

HOW DO THESE IDEAS (BUILT ON THE INSIGHT) SOLVE ALL THE PREVIOUSLY IDENTIFIED PROBLEMS/ OBSERVATIONS?

#1
It reduces or eliminates project creep.

With the portal, you're starting your home improvement project in a fundamentally different way. Instead of going to the store, you're uploading your photos without ever having to leave your house. People are already doing this anyway, on Facebook and in forums, but Facebook and forums aren't linked with a big box retailer like Home Depot or Lowe's. So while people may be getting advice from friends on social media or unvetted strangers in forums, they still have to buy those products elsewhere. By uploading your photo to the home improvement portal and getting an expert's advice, you'll save a ton of time and reduce (or even eliminate) project creep.

#2

It helps you do it like the pros.

After receiving your initial pictures and questions, those online experts can ask for additional pictures and clarification to get a better understanding of the problem and provide a more comprehensive solution. They can also start to educate you on the different DIY terms you need to know. The terms that they type into the chatbox can be linked to an online dictionary (a user-generated home improvement version of Wikipedia). That home improvement wiki could potentially link any project or topic to related pictures or videos for additional education as needed. Now, you're no longer calling things whatchermadoos and thingamabobbers like an amateur. You're talking more like a pro-fessional and there's minimal guesswork or translation needed.

#3

Save time with curbside or delivery.

Thanks to Covid-19, curbside delivery has become commonplace, even at home improvement stores, but the connective thread here is between the picture portal and the expert advice. The home improvement store can now bundle all the items you'll need, which you can easily order online at the end of your chat session so that you can pick up your items curbside or, better yet, have them conveniently delivered directly to your door in a branded truck, reminding everyone else in the neighborhood why they should shop at that home improvement store in the first place.

#4
Get more projects done.

As a result of this easy-to-use portal and the access you now have to certified experts, instead of approaching each project with fear or putting off certain projects for months, you actually *look forward* to tackling more projects. By having a distributed network of experts to answer your questions, the home improvement store can help you break through your inertia, carrying you from inspiration to action in a faster, more seamless process, transforming your home improvement "to-do" list into a "done" list so that you can spend more time in that hammock, watching your favorite sporting event or TV show in your beautifully re-designed screened-in, entertainment center-oasis-garden-cooking-area.

5

Data captured, projects optimized.

By starting each project with a picture and shifting more of the process online, the home improvement store can capture the data from all those conversations and develop a massive searchable database of information on projects, processes, and products. Compared to the one-on-one offline interactions that are happening in-store (and then evaporating into thin air as soon as they're done) the text, images, and videos from these conversations can be analyzed and optimized for even better processes and potential product innovations. (Observation #8 solved).

6

Store designs re-imagined.

Finally, by outsourcing the expertise component to the online network, the home improvement store can save money on how they staff and structure their warehouses, shifting layouts and operations to look more like IKEA in the front of the store (e.g. lifestyle vignettes) and more like Amazon in the back of the store (e.g. robots fetching products as online orders are placed).

Now can you see how the insight connects the dots of all those observations into a focused, actionable idea that solves those previously mentioned problems? I hope so. Because to me it's as clear as a constellation in the night sky.

A GREAT INSIGHT – BUILT ON A CONSTELLATION OF OBSERVATIONS, DATA POINTS, AND HUMAN TRUTHS – HAS THE POTENTIAL TO BUILD ENTIRELY NEW BUSINESS MODELS AND SOLVE SEVERAL PROBLEMS AT THE SAME TIME.

Keep in mind, I never said building the portal and developing a distributed network of experts would be cheap or easy, but I'm sure it wasn't cheap or easy to build the systems required for sites like AirBnB or HomeAway. That said, I believe that whoever ends up acting on this insight and pursuing this idea will become the category leader for a long time to come. I know plenty of people who would be ecstatic if they could sign up for a home improvement subscription service that was $9.99 a month to have access to certified experts who could provide remote one-on-one advice for all those tricky home improvement questions. Just think about how many underutilized experts are out there who could help people in need. With an online portal like this, built and branded by Lowe's or Home Depot or even Amazon, the home improvement category could be revolutionized.

* * *

The great thing about sharing these observations is that maybe for you, they've coalesced into an entirely different constellation, resulting in a different insight and a different set of ideas. That's awesome. That's the beauty of building insights as opposed to just finding them. You can take the same observations, add some more of your own, and then re-connect those dots in different ways, creating different images and ideas that you alone can see – an inspired glimpse into the future and how the world could be.

PART 3:

TECHNIQUES FOR BUILDING INSIGHTS

Bringing Method To The Madness

I wish I could say there's just one way to build an insight, but it's not like building a piece of furniture where all you have to do is follow a set of step-by-step instructions, and you'll have a beautiful insight every time. There are dozens of different starting places and techniques that people use to get to that "aha" moment when the stars align and everything becomes clear.

A lot of strategists will tell you there is no single process for building insights, and to some extent, I think that's true. Everyone brings their own "je ne sais quoi" to solving problems – a combination of personal life experiences that helps them see things a certain way. But underneath each strategist's idiosyncrasies and ability to connect the dots (which is definitely the most magical part of the process that's hard to teach or duplicate), there are a number of techniques that great strategists use to help them identify patterns and tune out the noise.

Here are some of those techniques.

Keep asking why.

At its most basic, this technique just requires you to take a data point, an observation, or a commonly held assumption and interrogate it with the same relentless curiosity as a 3-year-old.

→ Why aren't balloons edible?

→ Why don't bakers make bagel holes like donut holes and call them bagel balls?

→ Why is the word "big" smaller than the word small?

→ Why do we park in the *driv*eway?

→ Why are some people afraid to eat bugs?

→ Why are child car seat covers so hard to take off?

→ Why do you have to go to the store to try on glasses?

→ Why do vacuum cleaners have to be so bulky?

→ Why do moms use breast pumps in bathroom stalls?

There's a rebellious wisdom in questions that begin with why. That's because "why" challenges the status quo. "Why" asks for a reason, but sometimes those reasons can become outdated. Beginning your questions this way can be a powerful method for getting underneath your own preconceived notions about the category that you're trying to disrupt.

That's apparently what happened when Edwin Land was taking vacation photos with his family in 1947. His three-year-old daughter turned to him and asked, "Why do we have to wait for a picture?" As legend has it, that question was the spark that led to the Polaroid camera.

COMEDIANS ASKING WHY:

WHY ARE THE PICTURES SQUARE IF THE LENS IS ROUND?

- STEVEN WRIGHT, COMEDIAN
ALBUM: I STILL HAVE A PONY

MAMAVA

Why aren't there more places at malls, airports, or convention centers for nursing moms so that they can nurse their children or pump milk somewhere other than a bathroom stall?

That was the question that kept coming up again and again for Sascha Mayer, inventor of Mamava – a lactation pod for nursing moms when they're at work or public spaces.

The question first came up for Mayer with her own "undignified, demoralizing experience" as she describes it, of pumping milk in a restroom stall a few months after her son was born. She began seeing the same situation with new moms all around the country – women at work or in other public spaces nursing their babies or pumping milk in spaces that were never designed or intended to be "food prep" locations in the first place.

Then, on Labor Day in 2006, she came across an article in the *New York Times*, which showed a picture of a mom at work, preparing to pump, with a paper sign saying "Do Not Disturb" taped to the edge of her cubicle so that she could pump with some measure of privacy.

"Between my own experience and that picture in the *New York Times* - it all came together for me right there," Mayer says. "Why is breastfeeding - this thing which is fundamental to sustaining the human race - so unaddressed from a design perspective?"

On a more personal level, Mayer kept asking herself, "Why are these women so visible to me, but so invisible to everybody else?"

The answer that emerged: Because people who were traditionally in charge of designing public spaces (typically men) had made it invisible and because women had accepted it.

"Even things like breast pumps and the bags themselves," Mayer points out, "are in black bags, which are designed to be anonymous. Everything about breastfeeding has been designed to be invisible."

With that, Mayer had identified a pervasive problem that affected nursing moms everywhere, and her idea for Mamava began to take shape. However, it would take another six years before the first Mamava prototype was created.

Mayer admits, "Sometimes, you can identify the problem and have a great idea, but you need other factors to help push it along so that it can become a thriving business."

Between identifying the why and figuring out the how, there were several other stars that needed to align before Mamava could come to life, including:

New data – More and more studies showing the benefits of nursing, for mothers and their babies, which led to a growing movement of health and wellness around breastfeeding.

Legislation compliance – in 2010, with the Affordable Care Act, there was a compliance mandate that said if you have 50 or more employees, you have to provide lactation spaces.

Changing demographics – With Millennials eclipsing Boomers as the largest demographic in society and with more Millennials becoming parents, there began to be a bigger conversation around work and nursing and cultural expectations.

Social media – With more moms sharing their experiences publicly on social media, the problem of not having an adequately designed space for nursing and pumping had become more visible than ever before.

After several years and several prototypes, enter Mamava – an intentionally designed, comfortable space for nursing moms on the go.

As Mayer points out in her TEDx talk, everything about Mamava is designed to make the act of breastfeeding more visible, beginning with their happy breast logo.

Mayer continues, "The joyful nature of our freestanding lactation suites, with their curved walls and bright graphics telegraphed something new to the world – we weren't about *hiding* breastfeeding, but *celebrating* it - a solution for wherever moms go or work, which is, of course, everywhere."

So now that you know this technique, take some of those data points and trends that we identified earlier (that were inappropriately called "insights") and see where an infinite regression of "why" will take you. Or challenge everyone in the room to keep asking why and see where the conversation goes.

→ **Why is fast food usually so unhealthy?**

→ **Why are women their own worst critics?**

→ **Why do more households today have single people than married people?**

→ **Why is our trust in societal institutions waning?**

→ **Why aren't more Millennials saving for retirement?**

Any one of these questions has the potential to lead to a category-disrupting business or attention-getting campaign.

The trick with this approach, though, is that you can't just take the first answer and be done with it. You can't be afraid of conflict or offending someone. You have to keep pushing. You have to be insatiably curious and politely persistent. You have to be stubborn enough to *keep asking* why.

When asking why, you also have to challenge the commonly held belief that there's just *one* answer to the question. The truth is there may be a variety of reasons why people behave a certain way or why the culture is shifting in a particular direction.

When you're dealing with the tectonic plates of culture and the shifting sands of human behavior, there are usually dozens of reasons why things are the way they are. Your job is to line up all those reasons and come up with an insight that threads them together to create a new story or a compelling idea. Easy right?

IT'S HARD TO ASK WHY IN A SURVEY

Whenever I suggest focus groups or ethnographies to a client, they'll usually respond one of three ways.

 1. "That sounds expensive."

 2. "That's probably going to take a long time."

 3. "The population sample is too small."

Instead, they'll want to talk about surveys and statistically significant data. It's understandable. Surveys are faster. Surveys can reach a much larger population. Surveys let you slice and dice the data in numerous ways to help you find interesting patterns. For all these reasons, for most clients, surveys feel less risky.

The problem with surveys, though, is that they tend to answer a lot of "what" and "when" and "where" questions. They don't usually get to the why. Their inherent structure isn't built for that.

With surveys, you create the questions and a finite set of answers, which means you've already decided which answers are possible. You've eliminated any potential for someone to tell you something that's outside the scope of your own thinking.

Qualitative research techniques like focus groups, one-on-interviews, and ethnographies give you the opportunity to ask follow up questions and go deeper.

Why did you do it this way and not that way?

Why do you start your process like this?

What does that word mean to you?

You can't typically ask these kinds of open-ended questions in a survey because surveys need to be completed in ten minutes or fewer or else the respondent is going to experience survey fatigue and give up on the survey before they're done.

The truth is it's the stories people tell and the actual behavior that they engage in that can lead to those "aha" moments that get you closer to an insight.

That's exactly what happened when I was running a focus group for a national quick service restaurant chain. We were talking about healthy eating habits when someone in the group mentioned the idea of eating well. They said they liked to eat well and I asked them what that meant to them.

"What's the difference between eating healthy and eating well?" According to consumers, there's a huge difference.

"Eating healthy" implies an absence of flavor and an absence of fun. "Eating healthy" requires discipline. "Eating healthy" means eating meals like "naked" chicken and plain rice with steamed broccoli. "Eating well," on the other hand, can simultaneously include healthier, better-for-you options, while also implying flavor. "Eating well" can sometimes mean decadence, but there's more of a nuance to it than that. Eating well is about eating foods that are emotionally satisfying.

That's why I believe focus groups and interviews and ethnographies are, in some ways, better than surveys. Even though the population size is small, they give people an opportunity to tell you something you never could have imagined.

If you feel like asking "why" is too big a question or isn't taking you somewhere productive or practical, then try asking "why" in a different way. Start from the negative.

→ **Why aren't there showers at the airport?**

→ **Why aren't vacuums skinnier?**

→ **Why aren't people living up to their promises?**

→ **Why can't we call plant-based foods meat?**

That last one has been the driving question behind Beyond Meat's meteoric rise over the past several years. Instead of calling it a "meat alternative" or categorizing their products as "veggie" burgers that are tucked away in a different part of the store, Beyond Meat has challenged the traditional definition of what meat actually is. They've redefined the entire category by selling their plant-based burgers, meatballs, sausages, and chicken right next to "traditional" animal-based meat at many grocery stores (much to the dismay of the traditional meat industry).

When you stop and think about it, though, suggesting that plant-based meat be put in the same section of the grocery store as animal-based meat really isn't that unusual. After all, we use meat metaphors all the time to describe fruits and vegetables, and nobody thinks twice about it.

A **head** of lettuce.

An **ear** of corn.

Artichoke **hearts**.

The **eye** of a potato.

The **flesh** of the apple.

The **skin** of a peach.

The **heart** of the melon.

Why shouldn't plant-based products be sitting in the meat section? If it bleeds like meat, and it cooks like meat, and it tastes like meat, why can't we just call it plant-based meat?

We **should** be able to call it meat and that's exactly what Beyond Meat has done.

Here's another one of my favorite "why" questions:

WHY DON'T WE TREAT SCIENTISTS THE WAY WE TREAT ROCK STARS OR STAR ATHLETES?

That was the audacious "why" behind GE's campaign featuring Millie Dresselhaus, a real person who became known during her career as the queen of carbon science. The ad featuring Millie begins with a child unwrapping a birthday present, ecstatic to see that it's a Millie Dresselhaus doll. From there, we see kids dressed up as Millie Dresselhaus for Halloween, we see the real Millie being interviewed on a talk show, and we see a custom Millie emoji being shared by a student who just aced their physics test.

During the course of the ad, the narrator asks, "What if we treated great female scientists like they were stars? What if we lived in a world like that?"

The ad ends with this caption, "GE is helping create that world. Our goal is 20,000 women in technical roles by 2020."

It's a thought-provoking ad that positions GE as the hero, but the question they use could be leveraged by any number of other brands wanting to spark a movement.

Here's another "why" question that builds off that same premise:

WHY DON'T WE HAVE TELEVISION SHOWS ALONG THE LINES OF *AMERICA'S GOT TALENT,* BUT INSTEAD OF FEATURING SONG AND DANCE ROUTINES, WE COULD MEET ENTHUSIASTIC SCIENTISTS WHOSE DISCOVERIES AND INVENTIONS HAVE IMPROVED OUR DAY-TO-DAY LIVES?

I know what you're thinking. The reason a show like this doesn't exist is because scientists and mathematicians speak in hard-to-understand, multi-syllabic gobbledygook, which isn't very accessible to the general public. Dance routines play well on camera. Scientists — not so much.

But that's not really true. That's just a stereotype. There are a lot of charismatic, articulate scientists out there. Plus, if you give them a little coaching and some well-written cue cards, and you use those same flashy editing techniques to create vignettes that help them share their personal stories and why they got into science in the first place, we could potentially have the next hit show on our hands, sponsored by GE, Intel, Google, IBM, and so many other companies who are interested in cultivating the next generation of scientific breakthroughs. Netflix? Hulu? Amazon? Any takers?

* * *

As cliché as it may sound, when it comes to asking why, you have to question everything. You have to unlearn everything you think you know about how the world works. Don't accept the processes and parameters that are currently in use, because those processes may have been built a long time ago, with different technologies, different societal conditions, and a totally different mindset. You have to ask yourself how that product or service would be designed today if it were invented with today's technologies, today's constraints, or today's cultural norms.

These days, thanks to smartphones, faster Internet, video chat, augmented reality, and real-time inventory management systems, new businesses are popping up all the time that are finding new answers to the same basic question:

Why do I have to leave my house to _____?

→ **Watch a movie**

→ **Try on a pair of shoes**

→ **Try on glasses**

→ **Try on bras**

→ **Try out a mattress**

→ **Buy a car**

→ **Have a personal yoga/spin/crossfit trainer**

→ **Get groceries**

→ **Get basic medical advice**

So if you're looking for insights and innovation, keep asking why just like a three-year-old child until you, too, can see the world with a fresh set of eyes.

My daughter saw this sign outside a restaurant when she was three years old and asked me, "Daddy, does this mean no choo choo trains?" I have never seen this sign the same way since.

Create conflict.

"Americans think beans are boring, so how are we going to convince them to buy our product?" That's what the CEO of a national bean chip brand told me at our kickoff meeting.

Interesting perspective. Challenge accepted.

To get started on this project, I learned more than I ever knew before about beans, bean varieties, bean farmers, bean chip flavors, and how much fiber and protein was in a single serving of beans and bean chips respectively.

I reviewed numerous surveys with questions like:

* *How often do you buy XYZ brand of bean chips?*

* *Do you like the texture of XYZ brand of bean chips?*

* *How do our bean chips compare to corn chips?*

* *On a scale of 1 to 5, where 5 is "definitely" and 1 is "not at all" how likely is it that you would recommend our brand of bean chips to someone else?*

Even though I had answers to all of those questions, I kept coming back to the CEO's original assumption – Americans think beans are boring – and I wanted to figure out if that was true. So I developed a focus group discussion guide that would help me understand if there was any emotional resonance or deep feelings about beans to begin with (which sounds strange, I know).

Keep in mind, half the battle when it comes to great research is convincing your client that your line of questioning will yield something insightful. Since they have to approve the research methodology and the discussion guide in the first place, you have to think like a lawyer, creating a line of questioning that will simultaneously get approval from the client and build your case at the same time, so that you can get to the real heart of the issue.

With that in mind, as I built my discussion guide, I included several questions about snacking habits and healthy snacks and favorite flavors (questions I knew the client wanted to see), but the question I cared about most was, "Are beans boring or exciting?"

During the focus groups, I asked people to write their answers down on a piece of paper. Boring or Exciting. (With any controversial or conflict-driven topic, you want to make sure you get people to write their answers down first to avoid groupthink and bias during the discussion). Once they did that, I asked those who wrote down "exciting" to raise their hands. In group after group, there was consistently a 70/30 split in favor of people who thought beans were *exciting*.

Seriously. A lot of people out there have some really big feelings about beans.

So I asked the people who loved beans to explain to me and the rest of the group why they thought beans were so exciting. And then I asked them to try to persuade the other members of the group to see beans in a different light. It was almost like watching members of a jury trying to convince the remaining members to change their verdict. It was fascinating. There were debates and more than a few heated disagreements, but I never thought I would hear so many people talk so passionately about beans. How filling they were. How colorful. How versatile. Who would have thought beans could stir up so many emotions?

There were two ideas in particular that came together during these focus groups to create an "aha" moment for me.

First, in addition to saying beans are boring, the CEO had also mentioned how the bean category wasn't really known for innovation. He was right about that. Beans don't exactly have a reputation for making headlines.

Second, during our focus groups, everyone agreed that beans are *not* a convenient food group for people who lead busy lives and who are always on the go (no pun intended).

On the surface, both of these observations look like points in the negative column when it comes to marketing.

But when you combine these two ideas with the fact that this snack company had just transformed beans (a previously not very innovative category and a not-very-convenient "on-the-go" food item) into bean *chips*, well *now* you've got something interesting. You've got some tension. You've got a story of innovation. You've got all sorts of marketing messages that go beyond the basic product benefits of fiber and protein.

To be honest, there were so many "aha" moments during these focus groups, I could barely keep up. New headlines. New campaign directions. New flavor ideas. New product formats. All because we had created a healthy bit of conflict.

BRAND SPOTLIGHT:
VITAL FARMS

Vital Farms, the pasture-raised egg company based out of Austin, Texas, is no stranger to stirring the proverbial pot and generating conflict. In one of their first national campaigns, Vital Farms called bullshit on the cage-free egg industry. As the two-minute anthem spot opens, we see Stuart Dill, a real Vital Farms farmer talking to camera about how, "When it comes to eggs, there's a whole lot of cluckin' that doesn't mean much of anything." He mentions how other farms boast about being cage free. Then, with a sly grin and a spring in his step, he goes on to say how at Vital Farms, "Our pasture-raised eggs are bullshit free."

Of course, when you get to the heart of the campaign, you can see what Vital Farms is really doing is creating conflict, stoking a cultural conversation by challenging consumers to ask themselves a simple question, "What does cage-free actually mean?"

By using humor and some surprisingly frank language in their ads, Vital Farms effectively disarms consumers, suggesting that they look more closely at the living conditions of hens in cage-free environments vs. pasture-raised environments, which naturally leads people to a couple of disturbing facts. 1) Cage-free hens are indoors their entire lives. 2) Cage-free hens get about 1 square foot of space per hen. Compare those living conditions to the 108 square feet of space that each hen gets at Vital Farms and the winner of the argument is clear.

It's important to note that one of the biggest challenges when it comes to conflict-driven campaigns is the creative execution. There are a lot of ways Vital Farms could have tackled the issue of cage-free living conditions. B-roll footage of life indoors could have gotten really ugly really fast.

So be aware: if you're too earnest about the subject at hand or you don't hit that funny bone in just the right way, your campaign can end up being offensive or it can fall flat.

However, if you've got a powerful point of differentiation *and* you can land the punchline, you too can have a clever campaign that gets people talking.

One of the great things about a "conflict" group (as long as you can keep it civil) is that people often forget that they're in a focus group at all. They become so focused on their feelings about a particular subject that they start revealing thoughts and ideas that you never would have gotten out of them if you tried to steer clear of controversy. The real beauty of a conflict group is that when you share your findings with the client, even if those findings completely contradict the client's original assumption, it's not *you* disagreeing with the client (or in this case, the CEO). It's the voice of the people! It's the data from the research that they commissioned.

Remember, conflict is at the core of all great storytelling. Conflict is what gets characters to take action. Conflict is rich, fertile territory for insights because it's full of emotion. People will often tell you how they really feel about something even if they can't always explain why they feel that way. So the next time you're working on a project, see if you can create a dividing line to generate some healthy conflict. If so, you might be on your way to more insightful results.

> **CHALLENGING THE STATUS QUO REQUIRES EQUAL PARTS BRAVERY AND DIPLOMACY.**
>
> **YOU MUST BE BRAVE ENOUGH TO QUESTION EVERYONE'S PREVIOUSLY HELD IDEAS AND YOU MUST BE AS DELICATE AS A SEASONED DIPLOMAT.**

TECHNIQUE #3
Re-frame the question.

In research there's an old saying, "If you ask stupid questions, you'll get stupid answers." Or, to put it even more succinctly. "Garbage in. Garbage out." At the end of the day, the solution you're looking for is often baked into the question itself.

That's why I love this quote from Albert Einstein: "If I had an hour to solve a problem, I'd spend 55 minutes thinking about the problem and five minutes thinking about solutions."

In other words, how you think about the problem and how you frame the question will determine the kinds of answers and ideas that you come up with. It sounds simple enough, but existing frames and metaphors can be hard to break through sometimes. We often don't realize it, but our everyday conversations are *packed* with metaphors and those metaphors shape the way we see the world. In fact, that previous sentence is using a meta-phorical construct - conversations are like containers that are packed with these things called metaphors. Metaphors are like hands shaping clay. It's a real rabbit hole.

THE IDEA OF A FRAME IS IN, AND OF ITSELF, A FRAMEWORK.

THIS IS GETTING META.

When it comes to framing, here's the simplest example I know, which comes from Tina Seelig in her book *inGenius: A Crash Course on Creativity:*

What is the sum of {5+5}
vs.
What two numbers add up to {10}

The first question has just one answer. The second framing has multiple solutions. And that's the whole goal of re-framing – to take you out of a binary problem-solution framework so that you can see things in a different way and begin to notice other possibilities.

Here's the real trick, though. To re-frame a situation, you first have to be able to identify the initial framework. Most frames are invisible, so you have to get better at seeing those invisible frames in the first place. Since this is starting to sound like a metaphysical portal to a séance, let's stop talking about theories for a second and switch to some tangible business examples.

Frame #1:
"What can I help you find today?"

Retail employees in different categories ask this question all the time. It seems simple enough, but what they've accidentally done is trapped the customer into a framework whereby that customer is going to answer that question in the most binary way possible.

At a home improvement store, a home décor store, or an auto parts store, the customer might answer:

> "I'm looking for a drill bit."
>
> "I'm looking for a ceiling fan."
>
> "I'm looking for a spark plug."

The associate would then walk the customer to the aisle where they could find those items and that would be that. That would most likely be the end of the interaction.

A great salesperson, by contrast, frames their questions differently from the outset to get the customer to open up and share more information about their *real* purpose for coming to the store.

Frame #2:
"What project brings you in today?"

Both questions are about the same length, but the way they're framed can lead to totally different outcomes.

Now, instead of talking about a single item, the customer can start talking about their project. The story the customer tells may lead them to talk about several different items that they need. Instead of the employee just walking the customer over to the aisle where the item is located, the project-framing question opens things up to a much bigger *conversation*. By focusing on the project instead of the specific item, some customers can end up buying ten times as much product as they intended to buy in the first place. And it's not because they were duped. It's because the question-framing process revealed issues about the project that the customer didn't realize from the outset.

MOST OF THE TIME, EXISTING FRAMES CAN BE INVISIBLE. THEY'RE SO INGRAINED IN OUR WAY OF THINKING THAT WE DON'T SEE THEM. THAT'S WHY NOTICING THOSE FRAMES CAN BE THE FIRST STEP TO BREAKING THROUGH THEM.

Here's another example from the restaurant industry:

Let's say a recent customer survey highlights that 40% of your customers complain about the long lines to get into the restaurant.

This kind of data can lead to the assumption that the ordering process is too slow. That assumption can then lead to the following oversimplified framework:

Frame #1:
"How can we speed up our ordering process so that we can speed up the line and reduce wait times?"

It's not that this is a bad question. It's just that it's framing the problem in a particular way, focused on speed, which inevitably leads to the following solutions:

* *We should find ways to take orders faster.*

* *We should switch to a system of reservations instead of first come, first served.*

* *We should have a roving cashier go up and down the line and take orders with a mobile device.*

* *We should allow people to order online so they can skip the line entirely.*

* *We should streamline the menu so that customers don't have as many items to look at.*

* *We should yell at customers who are being too slow so that they'll order more quickly.*

All of these (except maybe that last one) are solid ideas and have been implemented at countless restaurants around the country.

But what if we frame the problem differently? What if we challenge the underlying assumption about standing in line, which is that people don't like to stand in line in the first place.

To break through frames, you have to start by asking, "Is that first assumption true? Are there ever situations where people stand around (not necessarily in a line) and enjoy themselves?"

The answer, of course, is yes. You bet they do. All the time. Go to any party and you'll see people standing around, chatting with each other without any complaints at all.

What are the conditions like in those situations?

For starters, they've usually got a beer or a glass of wine in their hands. There's music playing. There are snacks for people to munch on. There might even be some misters or an outdoor ceiling fan to keep them cool.

When you look at things this way, you might frame the problem a little differently: People are getting bored when they're waiting in our restaurant line. And with that new framework, you might end up with a very different question.

Frame #2:
"What can we do to make standing in line more enjoyable?"

With this new framework, the emphasis is no longer on reducing wait times, but instead on making the wait time more enjoyable and perhaps even memorable. That's a very different problem to solve, which can lead to a very different set of ideas, which might even lead to an entirely different business model or, at the very least, a competitive advantage.

* We could allow people to order beer, wine, or other beverages while they're standing in line. That way the wait will be more enjoyable because it will feel like they're just standing around with a bunch of friends in a more relaxed social context.

* We could put out a row of chairs or simple fold out stools so that people can sit if they want to, instead of standing.

* We could install a couple of televisions nearby so that people can be entertained while they wait.

* We could hire a musician or a comedian or a juggler to entertain our guests while they wait in line. This could lead to people taking videos of said entertainers while standing in line, tagging the location, and letting even more people know about the restaurant while at the same time giving more exposure to said entertainer.

* We could create an online trivia game for guests to play on their phones, with a chance to win points for correct answers, and the points can be redeemed for food, beverages, or branded merchandise.

Now before the restaurant chooses a solution, they should definitely run the numbers against each of these ideas and see which option is not only the most cost-effective way to solve the agreed upon problem, but which option might actually lead to even more exposure for the restaurant.

Again, it's not that the initial framing of the problem was wrong or that the second framing (and set of solutions) is so much better. The point is that a re-framed question leads to a fundamentally different set of solutions, which can sometimes be more cost effective *and* lead to multiple benefits or innovations.

When it comes to making wait times more enjoyable, theme parks have been some of the earliest innovators, using large television screens, animatronic characters, and interactive games to distract people from what would otherwise be a tedious experience, waiting in line for an hour or more.

The whole idea of re-framing suggests that we look at the problem from multiple angles and ask ourselves if there are circumstances when the problem we're having isn't a problem in other contexts. If not, why not? What can those other contexts teach us about the situation at hand so that we can come up with an unexpected, more innovative solution?

Here's another example from the world of lawn maintenance, highlighting how question framing can hide multiple assumptions:

How can we speed up the lawn mowing process?

The way this question is asked assumes, without explicitly stating it, that a *person* is involved in mowing the lawn, which then assumes that the person wants the chore of mowing the lawn to be done faster so that they can go do something else.

This "invisible" framework with all of its implied assumptions leads to all sorts of ideas for how to *speed up* the lawn mowing process.

But what if we take the person out of the equation? What if we stop assuming for a moment that a *person* needs to be involved when it comes to mowing the lawn? After all, there are now automated vacuum cleaners that don't require people. What happens to our framing of the question under these circumstances? What happens to the entire design of the lawn mower? First of all, it no longer needs a seat because we don't need someone to sit in it. If we don't need someone to sit in it, what happens to the rest of the design? Do we need a steering wheel anymore? What about the gear shift handle? Chances are, the weight and balance of the lawn mower will change significantly. With this design in mind, is *speed* the number one priority, or do you actually want the lawn mower to go *slower* so that the sensors can "see" the surrounding area and be more careful, avoiding dog toys or small children who might be playing in the yard? Kudos to Husqvarna for being brave enough to break through the standard frameworks and create their revolutionary robotic lawn mower.

Even simple questions can be loaded with hidden assumptions. It takes practice to recognize those assumptions, but once you get good at it, you'll get even better at re-framing questions, which will bring you one step closer to building a more effective insight.

BRAND SPOTLIGHT:
TROY PUBLIC LIBRARY

Troy, Michigan had an award-winning library that found itself in a bit of a budget crunch. To overcome their funding shortfall, the town of Troy scheduled a vote for a 0.7% tax increase to help provide the necessary funds to keep the library running.

Members of the community who didn't want to see a tax increase immediately started mobilizing and putting up lawn signs urging

---

people to vote NO on the proposed tax increase. In a short period of time, they quickly re-framed the conversation from one about books, libraries, and reading to an entirely different conversation that was focused exclusively on taxes. They used a classic framework where taxes are seen solely as a burden.

The standard response to this framework is to argue *inside* that framework, pointing out that taxes (and libraries) are not really a burden to the communities they serve because they come with all kinds of benefits, including free events and a more educated populace. Unfortunately, the problem with this argument is A) it's already trapped inside the existing framework (e.g. burden vs. benefit) and B) it's trying to convince an audience (the anti-tax group) that the library is relevant to them, even if they rarely use it.

It's a losing strategy because it's hard to convince an angry, organized, and motivated group to pay for something, in this case, libraries, that they don't think is necessary.

What's interesting in this case, though, is that instead of getting sucked into that existing "burden vs. benefit" framework in the first place, a group of people in Troy decided to try a new direction, re-framing the conversation completely by leaning into controversy, generating conflict, and creating signs that said this:

First, this idea caught the attention of people beyond the anti-tax group, people who are normally apathetic when it comes to local issues like library funding. Second, it obliterated the original frame by pushing the issue into a completely different value system — tapping into a deeply held belief that book burning is the hallmark of fascism. The idea of a book burning party made people angry. They shared pictures of the lawn signs on social media and they started debating the value of libraries and the audacity of burning books.

Within a matter of days, the conversation spread from social media to city council meetings, becoming not just a local issue, but one that was covered by international news outlets. When the conversation reached a fevered pitch, the group behind the campaign released their clever punchline:

A vote against the library is like a vote to burn books.

This powerfully re-framed idea led the yes voters — people who don't normally turn out to vote for run-of-the-mill issues like library funding — to turn out at levels that were more 300% greater than originally projected, and the proposition ended up winning by a significant margin, allowing the Troy Public Library to thrive.

To get to the promised land of insights, you have to be like a talented politician. You have to take the question that you've been asked and re-frame it into something that gets you to higher ground so that you can focus on the real problem at hand. It's not that you're trying to dodge the original question. You're just trying to re-examine the underlying assumptions that have been made. If you can't figure out those assumptions and hidden frameworks on the fly, then you'll have to ask your boss or your client for a moment or two (or maybe even a week!) to take a step back so that you can think things through.

It's hard to do, I know. Especially when you feel the pressure of those monthly or quarterly sales reports and everyone is running around with their hair on fire, trying to find new levers to pull to open up new streams of revenue. But based on all the interviews I've conducted, when I've asked people how they've gotten to great insights in the past, panic and fear were never mentioned as the emotional prerequisites.

So the next time someone accidentally or intentionally tries to trap you in a particular framework by asking you how you're going to generate more sales, you can start to shift the frame-work by saying something like this:

"That's a great question. I have a few ideas, but before I share them, let's see what we know about our customers first so that we can reach them more efficiently and talk to them more effectively, which should ultimately help us maximize sales."

With a framework like that, you're moving toward strategy instead of tactics. Now you're talking about audience demographics, psychographics, attitudes, and behaviors, which may get you to higher ground, which means you might be able to see more open sky, which means you might be closer to catching a glimpse of that constellation you've been looking for.

I know from firsthand experience that it can be hard to stay calm when everyone around you is anxious. In the high-stakes world of marketing and advertising, there is often a lot of money on the line, and a lot of people are looking to you for quick answers that will save the day. So do yourself a favor and make a sticky note that you can pin above your desk to remind you what to do during times like these. Or, if you're feeling really inspired, you can tattoo this mantra on your arm:

RE-VISIT THE SITUATION
RE-EXAMINE YOUR ASSUMPTIONS
RE-FRAME THE QUESTION

Look at the periphery.

Most of the time, businesses want to talk about themselves, but if you're trying to find something insightful, chances are, you'll have to look beyond the internal data that the business is providing.

Here's an example. Let's say you're working on a carpet brand and they're looking for an insight to help them sell their new line of stain resistant carpets. Chances are, your client has reams of data about carpet materials, competitive carpet brands, and different methods of carpet care. That's all good background information and those data points are important, but that information by itself probably isn't going to lead to anything that inspires an amazing creative campaign. That's because all the data is about carpet.

To get to something that resembles an insight, you need to go *beyond* the subject of carpets and carpet care and get to a universal human truth that's deeper than all of that. Then you have to connect the dots between the data and the truth and perhaps something else that you haven't even thought of yet.

IT MAY SEEM COUNTERINTUITIVE, BUT IF YOU WANT TO GET CLOSER TO AN INSIGHT ABOUT A PARTICULAR SUBJECT, YOU SOMETIMES HAVE TO ASK QUESTIONS THAT TAKE YOU FURTHER AWAY FROM THE SUBJECT AT HAND.

When it comes to carpets, you need to examine the concentric circles that surround the subject of carpets and carpet care. You need to widen your lens for a moment or two and look at subjects that are related to carpet care, but that are on the periphery.

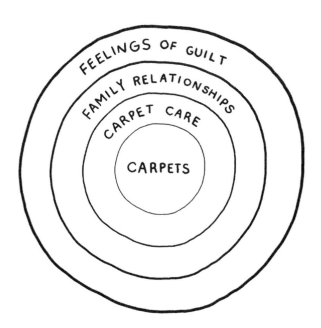

You need to ask people questions about their homes and about get-togethers and about family relationships. This particular line of questioning may drive your client crazy because all *they* want to do is talk about the unique selling proposition of their new stain resistant carpet, but if you want to go beyond the usual category conventions, you need to ask questions like a psychologist:

* *What does your home mean to you?*

* *What does a clean home mean to you on an emotional level?*

* *How much time do you spend cleaning your home before guests come over? Why is that?*

* *What are some specific things you do to clean your home (including your carpet) and why do you do some of those things that you mentioned?*

If you ask the right questions, you might land on something that's much bigger than carpet. You might begin to realize that when it comes to carpet care, people aren't just trying to get rid of a stain. They're trying to get rid of guilt. The stain is not what's on the floor. It's deeper than that. It's something you carry with you. It's that feeling you have when your mother is standing behind you, saying, "Honey. This (stain) just won't do."

Now I'm not saying that idea is an insight, but it's a lot closer to an insight than anything you might have had before, when you were looking at bar charts about carpet cleaning frequency.

It reminds me of a campaign for Tide to Go (Tide's stain removing stick) where a man is sitting down for a job interview with a small coffee stain on his shirt, and every time he attempts to answer a question or tell the interviewer a little bit more about himself, the stain on his shirt talks even louder.

Again, I'm not sure what the exact, pithy insight was for this campaign, but at the end of the day, it wasn't about the superior stain fighting properties of Tide to Go. There wasn't a timelapse demonstration of how quickly Tide to Go could eliminate stains from clothing. In fact, the ad never actually shows Tide to Go being used at all.

The obvious human truth is that stains are embarrassing, but the creative idea in the ad takes that truth to a more engaging level that everyone can relate to. Perhaps the insight behind the campaign is this: A stain isn't just embarrassing. It's distracting to the point of being obnoxious. A stain on your shirt says something about you that's louder than anything you're trying to say about yourself.

That idea is much more powerful than "stains are embarrassing," but it's too long. Remember, a great insight needs to be concise. So let's reduce it down by 90%.

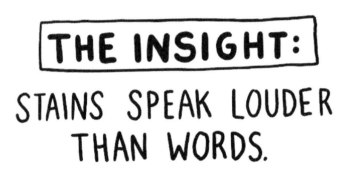

THE INSIGHT:
STAINS SPEAK LOUDER
THAN WORDS.

DOWNTOWN DOG RESCUE

Lori Weise, founder of Downtown Dog Rescue in Los Angeles, understands the power of looking at the periphery. Based on the research, she understood that 30% of dogs that enter a shelter are "owner surrenders," which means the dogs are deliberately relinquished by their owners.

However, instead of jumping to conclusions about the people who were relinquishing their pets to the shelter, Weise looked at other data sets – data that was previously on the periphery – and she used that information to shape their program. When looking at the situation through a wider lens, Weise discovered that "owner surrenders" are not a people problem. By and large they are a *poverty* problem.

As Weise explains, "These families love their dogs as much as we do, but they are also exceptionally poor. We're talking about people who in some cases aren't entirely sure how they will feed their kids at the end of the month. So when a new landlord suddenly demands a deposit to house the dog, they simply have no way to get the money. In other cases, the dog needs a $10 rabies shot, but the family has no access to a vet, or may be afraid to approach any kind of authority. Handing over their pet to a shelter is often the last option they believe they have."

With this in mind, whenever a family comes to Downtown Dog Rescue to relinquish their pet, a staff member starts by asking (without judgment) if the family would prefer to keep the pet. If the family answers yes, the staff member tries to better understand the root cause of the problem, leveraging the shelter's network and/or their knowledge of the system.

By approaching the issue from the periphery, Downtown Dog Rescue has found that 75% of families who come in wishing to relinquish their pets actually want to keep their pets. By focusing on a different set of data points and by changing their intake process as a result (e.g. asking different questions), Downtown Dog Rescue has managed to help more than 5,000 pets and families and has gained the formal support of the ASPCA.

So the next time you get stuck on a problem and you can't seem to find a way through, ask yourself the following question: "What are some issues with your business or your customers that might be worth taking a closer look at?"

Sometimes, just like when you're looking at stars, the stars can seem brighter and the pattern can reveal itself more when you're looking at the periphery compared to when you're looking directly at the problem itself. I know it sounds strange, but there are times when you have to look away to see things more clearly.

Interrogate language.

Words, words, words.

They can be so simple and yet they're filled with allusions, ambiguities, and complex shades of meaning. A single word or a simple phrase can start a riot or move people to tears because of how much history is attached to it.

Black.

What does it mean?

In the 1992 film, *Malcolm X*, there's a pivotal scene when Malcolm X, played by Denzel Washington, is asked by an inmate, "Did you ever look up the word 'black' in the dictionary?"

And so Malcolm X does, only to find the following definitions and associations:

Black:

Destitute of light.

Devoid of color.

Enveloped in darkness. Hence, utterly dismal or gloomy.

Soiled with dirt.

Foul.

Sullen.

Hostile.

Foully or outrageously wicked.

Indicating disgrace, dishonor, or culpability.

He also learns that the word black is used in many other words that have negative associations:

Blackmail.

Blackball.

Blackguard.

The inmate then prompts Malcolm X to look up the word white, where he discovers the following definitions and associations:

White:

Of the color of pure snow.

Reflecting all of the rays of the spectrum.

The opposite of black.

Free from spot or blemish.

Innocent.

Pure.

Without evil intent.

Harmless.

Honest.

Square dealing and honorable.

It's a powerful moment in the film, and it was probably an "aha" moment for Malcolm X as well, leading to several powerful speeches that shaped the culture and influenced generations of Black writers, musicians, artists, and apparently advertising professionals. More recently, this idea seems to have come full circle, with Proctor and Gamble urging dictionaries in 2019 to change their definitions of black as part of their "My Black is Beautiful" campaign.

* * *

Words and metaphors, with all of their associations, can shape how we see the world. (In fact, there's a metaphor right there, with words as tools and the world as a kind of clay sculpture.) That's why you have to interrogate words (metaphor) and look for the hidden frameworks (metaphor) that even the simplest phrases contain (metaphor), because those phrases can become the strategic foundation (metaphor) for a powerful insight.

According to James Geary, author of *I is An Other: The Secret Life of Metaphor and How it Shapes the Way We See The World*, in everyday conversation we utter about six metaphors a minute.

From politics:

Tax relief.

Grassroots.

Lame duck.

To everyday life:

Time is money.

Listen to your heart.

Life is a journey.

But when we recognize the metaphors that we're using and we consciously work to change those metaphors, we have the power to change the world.

That's why, if I were in politics, I would never offer a healthcare program with a name like "The public option." That's because of all the negative associations most people have with public things. Dirty public bathrooms. Underfunded public schools. Corroded public drinking fountains.

Whether you're in politics or strategic planning, if you're trying to inspire people, you have to choose your words (and your metaphors) very, very carefully.

COMIC INSIGHTS:
INTERROGATING LANGUAGE

George Carlin interrogates language to the extreme in his stand-up performance "Doin' It Again" (1990). When he gets to his diatribe about euphemisms, he points out how American English is loaded with euphemisms, and he explains why:

"Americans have trouble facing the truth, so they invent a kind of a soft language to protect themselves from it."

He points out that simple words or short phrases are typically closer to the truth and that the longer the phrase becomes, the more likely it's concealing something. He illustrates this by showing how in World War I, soldiers who came back from the war had experienced "shell shock" (two syllables). In World War II, the condition became known as "battle fatigue" (four syllables). After the Korean War, returning soldiers were diagnosed with "operational exhaustion" (eight syllables). And during the Vietnam War, the condition became known as "Post-Traumatic Stress Disorder."

As he explains, "Still eight syllables, but we've added a hyphen, and the pain is completely buried under jargon."

He goes on to point out how there are a number of other areas where language has changed over time.

Toilet paper became bathroom tissue.
The dump became the landfill.
House trailers became mobile homes.
Used cars became previously owned transportation.
And constipation became occasional irregularity.

Between government obfuscation, political correctness, and the work of advertising agencies, new and often ridiculous phrases are popping up all the time. So the next time you want to disrupt your category, take a closer look at some of those expressions, interrogate the words and the ideas they're trying to hide, and you might be one step closer to an insight.

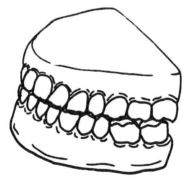

Are these false teeth or dental appliances?

A lot has been written about metaphors in politics, but as we can now see, metaphors are everywhere, and they're used all the time in marketing and advertising copy.

Your home is your castle.
The future is ahead.
Fall in love.

To get closer to a category-disrupting insight, every one of these metaphors (and their hidden assumptions) should be challenged.

What else is a home other than a castle?
Can the future be behind you?
Is love something that we fall into?

The idea of "falling in love" is especially interesting in an increasingly algorithm-driven world, because the hidden idea underneath the phrase "falling in love" is that it happens by chance. You "fall into" love. You walk around a corner one day and stumble into the love of your life. How many movies and stories over the years have reinforced that idea? How many of us believe in our heart of hearts that "Love just happens"?

But what if we interrogated that phrase a little bit more? What if, instead of accepting the idea that love is a random event that happens to the lucky few, we looked more closely at the idea of compatibility and algorithms?

What if an online dating site dug deeper into those ideas and proposed (no pun intended) that love is not something that you fall into, but it is something that can be calculated? I know that's not exactly romantic (our culturally accepted idea of romantic love is that it isn't supposed to be calculated or calculating), so I'm not saying that should be the headline in the final ad campaign, but I definitely think there's something that's close to an insight here.

As Tony Morrison wrote in her award-winning novel, *Jazz*, "Don't ever think I fell for you or fell over you. I didn't fall in love. I rose in it."

Sometimes, a provocative quote or passage from literature, film, or television can challenge our common metaphors and be the inspiration for a powerful new insight. You just have to keep your eyes and ears open.

Find the contradiction.

It's no secret that a lot of great insights and creative campaigns tap into cultural tensions. Those tensions can often be found in contradictory messages that permeate the culture.

Just look at the beauty industry as it relates to women. On the one hand, there are messages out there telling girls and women that "it's who you are on the inside that counts" or "just be yourself." On the other hand, there are several overlapping multibillion dollar industries, including cosmetics companies, skincare, hair care products, and personal hygiene products that suggest in subtle and not-so-subtle ways the opposite message – that beauty is really just skin deep, and you should groom, pluck, curl, straighten, and powder your way to a better life.

To put it more simply, these industries have created an unrealistic and unattainable standard when it comes to beauty. From the picture-perfect models to the studio lighting to the incredibly sophisticated photo-retouching software that takes away every pimple, stray hair, and blemish, there is no way the average human being can ever look as good as they do in the ads. It's not physically possible and everyone knows it.

It was this cultural contradiction – this tension – that served as the springboard for Dove's award-winning *Campaign for Real Beauty*, which has been challenging cultural norms, sparking tough conversations, and going strong in one iteration or another for more than a decade, highlighting women of all shapes, sizes, and skin tones, with and without freckles, tattoos, or grey hair.

And while the Dove campaign was grounded in a landmark global study on women, beauty, and well-being, you don't necessarily need a multi-month ethnographic study to highlight cultural contradictions.

In today's world, where you can find an editorial on either side of the political or cultural spectrum, you can find contradictions almost anywhere. In fact, a quick perusal of social media conversations can reveal a host of contradictory aphorisms that have been around forever.

WHICH ONE IS TRUE?

If you want something done, you've got to do it yourself.

VS

If you want something done, you should outsource it.

- -

Good things come to those who wait.

VS

Good things come to those who take charge.

- -

Absence makes the heart grow fonder.

VS

Out of sight, out of mind.

- -

You're never too old to learn.

VS

You can't teach an old dog new tricks.

- -

Birds of a feather flock together.

VS

Opposites attract.

On the surface, every one of these aphorism pairs seems contradictory, but in reality, they're not. In every case, both aphorisms are true, but they're true under different circumstances. When you look more closely at the contradictions, you may find some surprising things, which can bring you closer to the insight you're looking for. Finding the contradiction can sometimes begin with interrogating language, but more often than not, it comes from observing the world around you, listening carefully to people's complaints and trying to understand the patterns and subtle nuances between one situation and the next.

After all, how can obesity be on the rise in the United States and yet there are so many weight loss books, apps, and places to work out? How can the Internet, which was supposed to usher in an era of radical transparency, be riddled with so much disinformation? Why is it that people claim to feel more alone than ever before even though there are so many social media platforms designed to foster connection?

Somewhere inside these contradictions there are truths, new business ideas, and engaging campaigns just waiting to be found.

CAPITALIZING ON CONTRADICTIONS
LAY'S "DO US A FLAVOR" CAMPAIGN

Consider this confluence of conflicting data points:

1. Flavor is the #1 consideration when buying a snack.
2. People are afraid to buy new or unusual flavors.
3. New or unusual flavors get people talking on social media.
4. Unusual flavors are unlikely to sell at scale and are a major risk when it comes to new product launches.

What's a brand to do?

Almost any survey in the consumer-packaged goods category will tell you that flavor is the number one reason why people will eat snacks or try new snacks from a familiar or an unfamiliar brand. Year after year, in the Mintel Snacking Motivations and Attitude Survey, when respondents are asked, "Which of the following are important to you when choosing a snack?" flavor is always the leading choice. After flavor usually comes (lowest) price, calorie content, and brand, but flavor is almost always in the lead by a margin of two to one over price.

But that's not the only data point to consider. Social media data mining across the salty snack category would undoubtedly highlight the following:

- New flavors have a tendency to get people talking, and certain popular flavors specifically lead to increased levels of fan engagement on social media.

- The more unusual the flavor is, the more engagement you get as people comment and get into heated debates.

- Flavors that might be unusual in one culture may be extremely popular in another culture, thus opening up new opportunities to expand market share in other countries or specific regions.

- If consumers have had a role in coming up with a new flavor idea, then they are more likely to engage with the brand on social media (e.g. liking, commenting, or sharing) because they want their friends and family to know that they were the ones who came up with the idea in the first place.

So on the one hand, the data seems to be in favor of launching new and unusual flavors, but there's still the risk of launching a flavor that might not get mainstream adoption. As innovative as the food scientists are at Lay's in coming up with new and unusual flavor ideas, I'm sure there were market researchers who discouraged them after asking the following (common) survey question:

On a scale of 1 to 5, where 1 is not at all likely and 5 is extremely likely, how likely would you be to purchase the following flavor of potato chips?

> Flamin' hot dill pickle
> Cappuccino
> Grilled Cheese and Ketchup
> New England Lobster Roll
> Wasabi Ginger
> Chicken and Waffles
> Everything Bagel with
Cream Cheese
> Mango Salsa

> Bacon Mac & Cheese
> New York Reuben
> Indian Tikka Masala
> Southern Biscuits & Gravy
> Korean Barbecue

No doubt, most people would answer "not at all likely" for the majority of these flavors. In this way, because of how the question is asked, the data can sometimes lie.

To *disrupt* the snack category, you have to approach the question of flavor from a different angle. You have to go deeper than a survey will allow and give people room to tell their stories. For instance, here's a data point about flavor that I've seen come out of people's "snacking stories" in focus groups time and time again.

WHEN PEOPLE BUY A CHIP FLAVOR THEY'VE NEVER TRIED BEFORE, THEY ALSO TEND TO BUY A "BACK UP" BAG OF A FLAVOR THEY DO KNOW.

Instead of running away from this paradox of data points, Lay's leaned into the tension between the known and the new. Instead of keeping the R&D flavor ideation process a secret and then spending millions of dollars on taste panels, focus groups, and surveys, followed by one potentially risky launch campaign after another, Lay's turned that entire new product lifecycle into one big marketing campaign, rewarding the creator of the most popular flavor with either one million dollars or 1% of that year's net sales (whichever was greatest).

Not only has the Lay's campaign/contest been running for several years in a row, creating hundreds of millions of impressions each year, it has also resulted in more than a dozen new flavors that were essentially pre-approved before they launched.

By tapping into the tension between this paradox of data points, Lay's managed to maximize the talk value of new and unusual flavor ideas (putting Lay's at the center of the cultural conversation) while minimizing the fear of new and unusual flavors.

When you combine these data points with the nimble, customizable manufacturing capabilities and digital wherewithal of Lay's (e.g. partnering with Facebook in their first year of the "Do Us a Flavor" campaign to customize Facebook's standard "like" button with an "I'd eat that" button), it makes perfect sense for Lay's to ask their fans to come up with new flavor ideas and turn the whole thing into an annual contest.

Sometimes, contradictions can cause dissonance. In this case, though, Lay's found harmony in the dissonance and turned those contradictions into a multi-million-dollar idea.

* * *

Behind every great business idea and every great campaign, someone had the courage to lean into the contradiction, look into the eye of the tornado, and see things that no one else was able to see. Ultimately, if you want to build a category disrupting insight, you can't just ignore the contradictions in the culture or throw your hands up in the air and say, "It just doesn't make sense!" You have to dig into the details, find the devil, and wrestle with him.

Ask "what if" more often.

If asking "why" is the root of motivation, then asking "what if" is the root of imagination.

Because that's what insights are really all about. Imagination. Connecting the dots in new ways. Seeing an idea or an exciting new future that no one else can see. Imagination, one of human-kind's greatest gifts, is the ability to conjure up new worlds and new possibilities with two simple words: "What if...?"

Kids ask "what if" questions all the time because, as the old saying goes, they don't know any better. Of course, that old saying assumes that we, the grown ups, *do* know better. But what if we don't? What if our idea of better isn't actually better? What if we took a moment to forget everything we thought we knew about how the world works and we asked more "what if" questions instead? How different would the world be?

I know that in boardrooms and business meetings, "what if" questions can seem like a waste of time, but asking "what if" questions can often be one of the most effective ways to get people to break out of their comfort zones and come up with disruptive new ideas.

FROM THE PHILOSOPHICAL:

- What if God were a She?
- What if time isn't moving forward, but backward?
- What if there are more than five senses?

TO THE WHIMSICAL:

- What if we let our children be in charge of making dinner for a week?
- What if we didn't pack suitcases for our next vacation?
- What if everyone on earth stopped talking for a day?

TO THE WORLD OF BUSINESS:

- What if we didn't need fire to cook food? (Hello microwaves!)
- What if cars could drive themselves? (Hello driverless cars!)
- What if we let strangers sleep in each other's homes? (Hello homesharing!)

Asking "what if" is exactly what Nissan did for their campaign featuring the Nissan Leaf. The ad begins by showing a number of household and workplace items that normally run on electricity now running on gas. Cell phones. Coffee makers. Computers. Copy machines. Everything has a tailpipe and an internal combustion engine. It's an alternate universe that seems absurd, and yet you can't look away, especially when a dentist fires up a gas-powered drill like a lawn mower to work on someone's tooth.

"What if everything ran on gas?" the narrator eventually asks. The answer also comes in the form of a question. "Then again, what if everything didn't?" And that's when you see the Nissan Leaf, the 100% electric, zero gas car that is the hero of this parallel world and our own world, a symbol of innovation for the planet and innovation for all.

It's a powerful ad, but I think Nissan (or any electric car company) could have taken that "what if" line of questioning a few steps further. Instead of just telling people on their website and in press releases that most commutes (urban or rural) are less than 100 miles per day, Nissan could have created additional innovations and a more robust pipeline of potential new customers based on the following "what if" questions.

What if Nissan created a free mobile app that anyone could download so that they could keep track of their daily commute so that they could see the commuting data for themselves? After a period of time, with the data in hand, Nissan could offer them incentives to trade their current car for a Nissan Leaf.

Furthermore, what if, on those rare occasions when Nissan Leaf owners needed to go more than 100 miles, Nissan had a car rental program that allowed Nissan Leaf owners to rent another car for free or for a small fee, the same way that some banks wave the cost of the transaction fee at other ATMs? How many more people could Nissan speak to and learn from if they pursued this "what if" data-centric line of questioning?

The most powerful thing about "what if" questions is that they don't have preset answers. They require you to see the world with a fresh set of eyes. On the one hand, that's what makes them daunting for most organizations, but on the other hand, that's also what makes them so powerful.

So what if you came to your next brainstorm meeting with more "what if" questions? How many new ideas or potential new insights might you build?

DOLLAR SHAVE CLUB ASKS "WHAT IF?"

For years, Gillette had dominated the men's shaving category. But their signature approach to innovation, it seemed, was to just add another blade. Eventually, this got the attention of *The Onion*, which in 2004 released a prescient article poking fun at the shaving giant with the headline, *"Fuck Everything. We're Doing Five Blades."*

We'll never know if that satirical piece was the original spark that led to the rise of Dollar Shave Club in 2011, but I guarantee you the provocative question at the center of their business model began with two words: What if? What if we looked at innovation from a different angle? What if, instead of just adding more blades to our razors, we innovated around the buying process? What if, instead of making people buy razor blades at brick-and-mortar stores, we allowed people to buy their razor blades online, as a subscription?"

It turns out their answer to those "what if" questions paid off, because in 2016, just five years after its launch, Dollar Shave Club sold to Unilever for $1 Billion.

What if by asking "what if" your brand could do the same?

PART 4:

HOW TO SELL AN INSIGHT

YOU HAVE AN INSIGHT. NOW WHAT?

Congratulations! After steeping yourself in data, trend reports and your own personal observations, and after using different techniques to build insights – asking "why" and "what if" questions, creating conflict in focus groups, and finding subtle nuances in contradictory data points – you finally have an insight. An absolutely game-changing, campaign-worthy, category-disrupting, business-building insight.

Or at least you think you do.

You've double-checked your insight against the checklist so you know it contains a universal human truth, it's backed by data, and it's got some tension. Plus, you've tightened the language down so now it's nice and pithy. You're feeling really good about it.

What should you do with it? Should you run to your client, your CMO, or your creative director and say, "Stop what you're doing and listen to this insight! It's going to change EVERYTHING!"

No. Absolutely not.

You have to remember that you've been thinking about this for days, weeks, months, or even years. The people you're about to share this with haven't been thinking about these things at all. Or, at least not in the same ways that you have. They haven't had a chance to connect all the data dots and observations and human truths that you've been organizing and reorganizing in your head, so if you tell them your insight without the proper setup, they're going to look at you as though you just read them an impromptu haiku. Chances are, there will be a moment of silence after you're done sharing your precious insight as they absorb the information, and then they'll nod their heads and say, "That was interesting. Thank you for that." And they'll go back to doing whatever they were doing before you burst into the room.

So what should you do?

First, before you take it to the "higher ups," you need to gut-check your insight with someone whose opinion you really trust. That's because an insight, when it's brand new, is a lot like a baby seal. It's vulnerable. It's still a little wet behind the ears. If it's not truly ready for the world, there are people out there who will be more than happy to club it to death instead of giving it a chance. It's nothing personal. Insights just have a way of making people aggressive. It's weird.

So if you have a friend or a colleague who loves to nerd out with you about human behavior and data and solving big business problems, and you know they won't take your idea and repackage it as their own, then the first thing you should do is share your fledgling little insight with them so that they can gently poke at it with a stick instead of immediately decapitating it with a samurai sword. Stress testing your insight is how you'll make your insight even better. It'll get bruised, and so will your ego, but the bruising will make your insight stronger, which will ultimately make it stand up taller, which is necessary for it to really stand out.

But even before you take the insight to your friend, confidant, or favorite colleague, you still have to work on your setup. Because at the end of the day, selling an insight is all about storytelling. You have to line up your plot points in an organized, compelling way so that your friend can follow along, and perhaps more importantly, they can't wait to hear what's next. Like any great storyteller, you have to have a good hook, great pacing, and just the right number of clues to keep your audience on the edge of their seats, simultaneously listening to you and trying to solve the mystery with you. If the premise isn't believable or interesting enough, or if the pacing isn't right, then you'll lose your audience before you get to the big reveal.

To be honest, selling an insight can be one of the most challenging parts of the entire process. That's because most people in the corporate world have the attention span of a gnat. It's not their fault. Between meetings, text messages, quarterly profit reports, and hair-on-fire requests from one department or another, that's just the way things are. So you have to prepare your facts and pace out your plot twists like someone who's writing a thriller.

In other words, having the insight alone isn't enough. A big part of your job as an Account Planner or Chief Insights Officer is developing a variety of engaging storytelling methods so that people will come along for the ride and, most importantly, hang on to your every word.

As Nancy Giordano, one of the world's leading futurists, shared with me during an interview:

"Here's the thing. The process of asking all these questions and tracking the information down is a lot like going into a jungle. Since I've been doing this for a long time and because I'm a good navigator, I'm able to figure out the path that will take me out of the jungle to the top of the mountain, where the insight can be seen. But there are so many learnings that come from that process of going through the jungle – which berries are poisonous and which ones aren't, which trails lead to dead ends and which ones get to higher ground – and those learnings are part of what forms the insight."

It's true. Sometimes, though, a client can get impatient and ask you to fast-forward to the mind-bending conclusion. However, if you do that – if you share the insight without the necessary setup, the client won't appreciate the insight. Chances are, they won't even know what they're looking at or how to process the information. It's like saying the punchline to a knock-knock joke without first saying "knock-knock." As simple as that setup is,

"Knock-knock" followed by "Who's there?" is the world's oldest and shortest storytelling hook – it creates tension, which is what makes the punchline so satisfying (if it's a good punchline). That's why your setup is so critical. After all, how can you reveal the plot twist to a story without first setting up the characters, the setting, and the situation? You can't. A murder mystery without the mystery is just murder.

In other words, when it comes time to selling your insight, you've got about five to ten minutes to boil down the hundreds of hours of reading, data analysis, and thinking that you've been doing for the past several months. That means you don't get to share the director's cut. There's no time for a feature length film. You've got to tell your story with the heart and soul of a Pixar short.

No pressure, right?

So with that in mind, here are some techniques I've learned over the years from mentors, screenplay writers, and other amazing human beings for how to tell (and sell) a great story.

ACT 1: HOOK YOUR AUDIENCE

In the publishing world, literary agents and editors will read just one or two pages before they decide to keep going or not. On YouTube, the data shows that you typically have fewer than five seconds to get and hold someone's attention before they move on. In a presentation, you have about one slide. So the question is, if you're using slides at all, what are you going to say on that first slide to get (and hold) people's attention?

Start with an unbelievably compelling data point.

Most presentations have too much data in the body of the presentation instead of in the appendix where it belongs. If you include any more than 3-5 data points in your presentation (let alone on a single slide) chances are you'll lose your audience. So instead of dumping a hundred mind-numbing data points across a couple dozen slides, choose one unbelievably compelling data point and let it fill the slide as a way to start your story. That's a much better way to get someone's attention, and chances are, they'll give you permission to tell them more.

Here's an example:

1 million people

die every year

from malaria.

If that's not compelling enough, you can always reframe the data in different ways, depending on your audience.

3,000 CHILDREN

die EVERY DAY

from malaria.

The thing to keep in mind if you use a data point to open your presentation is that the data point has to be so extreme that it's almost unbelievable. I know that sounds like a risky move, but the data you share has to be shocking enough to make someone do a double take. That's also why it's important to cite your data clearly, preferably from a credible source. That way if someone asks, "Can that be right?" you can point to the source and keep moving. (By the way, my source for the data points above come from Unicef.org from their malaria fact sheet.) The old axiom is true:

people remember stories, not data. But sometimes, the right data point can be an amazing way to hook people in.

Compare things with a powerful juxtaposition.

Juxtapositions are another great way to create tension and make people understand just how much the world has changed, which can quickly pave the way to the insight you want to show them. Often, you can create an amazing juxtaposition with data. Other times, a split-screen photograph with a little bit of voice over can be all it takes to get someone's attention. The trick, of course, is finding those two things that will make your audience stop in their tracks (or put down their phones) and look at you with an expression that says, "You have my full attention. Please continue."

Once, when I was working on a presentation for a job recruitment company, I needed to highlight how competitive the modern workforce had become. To start, I used a juxtaposition: one slide with two resumes side-by-side. The first resume, on the left, was a real resume from the 1980s – it was clearly made on a typewriter it mentioned marital status, and it filled up about half the page. The other resume, on the right, was so full of accomplishments, accolades, and extra-curricular activities, that the margins had to be reduced to a quarter inch on all sides to fit everything in.

Of course, I could have started off with bar charts and graphs and all kinds of data points, but sometimes a simple "Then & Now" or "Before & After" approach can say far more and be far more impactful than all the data points in the world.

Make it personal.

If you have an experience from your own life that ties back to the insight, then start with your story – even if that means getting a little personal. Sometimes, that vulnerability can make your audience lean in just a little bit more.

Daniel Pink does this extremely well in his TED talk. Here's how he starts: "I need to make a confession at the outset here. A little over twenty years ago, I did something that I regret, something that I'm not particularly proud of. Something that, in many ways, I wish no one would ever know, but here I feel kind of obliged to reveal."

What's he going to say next? Everyone wants to know. Like a

good comedian, though, he goes on to reveal that the thing he regretted doing as part of his youthful indiscretion, was going to law school. Well played, Daniel Pink. Well played.

Of course, your personal story doesn't necessarily have to have a punchline. People love an unexpected twist, but it doesn't have to be a comedic twist. The point is to make a connection with people so that they'll be leaning in with anticipation, curious to know what comes next.

Use a physical object.

No. Not like Al Capone did with a baseball bat in the film *The Untouchables*. You're going to have to be more subtle than that. Most people go into presentations expecting to be bombarded with a series of charts and stats and quotes – everything that can be projected onto a screen. But you're not like most people. You have a category-disrupting insight! So why not disrupt the normal presentation procedure in the first place? Sure, you can still have slides, but why not hook people in with a three-dimensional object that they can hold or open or smell? Surprise them with something more tactile so they understand that this is a different kind of presentation that will lead to a very different kind of outcome.

Bill Gates does a masterful job of getting and holding people's attention during his TED talk about malaria by combining a compelling data point, a humorous juxtaposition, and by using live mosquitoes. First, he points out that there's more money invested into baldness drugs than into malaria drugs. Wow. That's a crazy data point. Then he follows that unbelievable statistic with a humorous juxtaposition. "Now baldness is a terrible thing," he says, while the audience laughs at the absurd comparison. Then, he opens a jar filled with mosquitoes and says, "Now malaria is, of course, transmitted by mosquitoes. We'll let those roam around the auditorium a little bit." While many of the audience members are still laughing, if you look closely at the expressions on some of their faces, you can see how this experience is being burned into their psyches. Ultimately, he tells the audience that those mosquitoes are not actually infected with malaria, but I'm sure that no one in that auditorium has ever forgotten that experience.

ACT 2: TAKE THEM THROUGH THE JUNGLE (QUICKLY)

As I mentioned earlier, you can't just jump to the insight or the final answer without going through the jungle first. Otherwise, your audience won't recognize the insight when they see it. So the trick is to make the journey as exciting and as enjoyable as possible so that they stick around until the very end. That means you've got to organize your story like a binge-worthy television show, creating a series of cliffhangers that get people sitting on the edge of their seats, eager to see what's next.

As any great storyteller will tell you, it all comes down to a few simple elements: characters, pacing, and plot twists. The characters in this story are your customers or the people who influence the decision-making process. The plot twists are the things you've discovered through your research – amusing anecdotes, compelling yet contradictory behaviors – moments of dissonance when someone says one thing but ends up doing the exact opposite.

Editing is everything.

This is where your nerdy friend can be a huge help, because they'll be able to tell you honestly where they're getting lost or bored. Of course, you'll be tempted to keep certain slides, stubbornly insisting they include sacrosanct nuances, but when your friend suggests that you cut these slides, listen to them. If you can keep the heart of your story down to just 5-10 slides with a combination of pictures and pithy headlines, chances are you'll be able to keep your audience hooked for the grand finale.

Make the data visual.

It's one thing to have data, or even big data, at your fingertips. It's another thing to harness that data and transform it into a compelling data safari. That's where data visualization tools can come into play and turn your presentation into an action-adventure story. When you combine a hypothesis with organized data and maybe even a timelapse video that shows how the data transforms over time, you can literally connect the data-dots in real time for people so that they can't turn away.

Show them, don't tell them.

Executive summaries are all the rage in boardrooms and creative briefings, but sometimes an executive summary can lose its power, because an executive summary is all about summarizing key points instead of showing first-hand experiences. Sometimes hearing people speak in their own words can be more moving than a summary will allow. This is where having the skill set of a video journalist or a documentary filmmaker can be valuable, because you can pull together powerful moments and sound bites that can persuade your audience to see things differently.

Back in the day, when I was an Account Planner in New York City there was a presidential election coming up where both candidates kept talking about the American dream. I couldn't help but notice that one candidate was in his seventies and the other candidate was in his forties, and I had a hunch that their respective supporters had different ideas of what the American dream was all about. So over the course of two weekends, I went to Union Square and asked people of different ages, nationalities, and backgrounds to tell me what the American dream meant to them.

This resulted in a two-minute video, which we ultimately shared with our roster of clients to talk about the changing nature of the American dream, evolving expectations, and the importance of brand evolution.

Sometimes it can be helpful to let other people say things in their own words, because they'll deliver their stories in a far more personal and compelling way than you could ever summarize.

ACT 3: THE BIG REVEAL

**"The ending of a play or novel should be
surprising yet inevitable."
-Anton Chekhov**

Revealing the insight can be a lot like the biggest plot twist in a film. That's what makes some books and movies more memorable and talk-worthy than others. But how do great storytellers do it? How do they reveal the truth that's been hiding in plain sight the entire time? That's what you'll need to master if you are to be known as "The Insightful One."

In the vast majority of books, films, and TV series, the biggest plot twists are often tied to identity. (Warning: spoilers ahead, but most of them are so popular you've probably already seen them.)

* *In The Crying Game, we learn at the end that she is a he.*

* *In Fight Club, we find out that Edward Norton's character (the unnamed narrator) and Brad Pitt's character (Tyler Durden) are one and the same.*

* *In The Usual Suspects, we spend 98% of the film wondering, "Who is Keyser Söze?" only to find out in the last few minutes that it was the person being interrogated the entire time - the seemingly innocent Roger "Verbal" Kint (played by Kevin Spacey).*

* *In The Sixth Sense, we never suspect that Bruce Willis' character (Malcolm Crowe) is a ghost, even though Haley Joel Osment's character (Cole Sear) tells him very early on, "I see dead people."*

* *In Psycho, we discover that Norman Bates developed a split personality after he killed his mother and started dressing up like her to kill certain guests at the Bates Motel. (That's a tough business model!)*

In some cases, the main character doesn't actually know who they are themselves. Yet because of the pacing, the action sequences, and some clever dialogue, we hang on for the ride.

Check out *The Bourne Identity*, *Shutter Island*, or *Westworld* as examples. In the movie *Memento*, we experience the world through the eyes of Leonard Shelby (played by Guy Pearce), who suffers from anterograde amnesia, which results in short term memory loss. The first three minutes of the film are disorienting as things go in reverse: a Polaroid picture showing a homicide scene, fading to white like a memory being erased. Then we cut to Leonard Shelby in a motel room, wondering how he got there. As the audience, we're just as confused as he is, but we're given the right number of clues at the right intervals to keep us hooked and wanting more.

When you look at what all of these stories with plot twists have in common, it's pretty simple: people are not who we think they are. They're much more nuanced than that, and some of the most exciting stories reveal those complexities in compelling ways – using snippets of dialogue, flashbacks, black and white footage, music, and more. As David Ogilvy once famously said, "The consumer is not a moron. She's your wife." In other words, we need to break free of our knee-jerk assumptions about people because they are often more complex than we realize at first glance.

What every great story really does is it takes the main character and the audience on a journey of self-discovery. A great story reveals something (or perhaps many things) about the character, and if it reveals something true about the human condition (the universal human truth), then we, as the audience, discover something about ourselves as well.

And that can be transformative.

In *The Matrix*, which is an impressively layered metaphor, the entire story is a series of revelations. First, Neo realizes he's in a computer simulation called the matrix. That's a tough pill to swallow. (Pun totally intended.) Then, with that understanding, he realizes he can jump between buildings and move faster than he ever thought possible. From there, he trains with Morpheus to "fight" against the agents, which is, perhaps intentionally, a misleading framework.

In a pivotal scene in the first half of the film, Morpheus explains to Neo how everyone who has ever fought an agent has died and that's because their strength and their speed is based in a world that is built on rules. "Because of that," Morpheus concludes, "they will never be as strong as you will be." To which Neo asks the single most important (and revealing) question of the film, which is tied to the culminating plot twist at the end. "What are you trying to tell me?" Neo asks. "That I can dodge bullets?" To which Morpheus replies, "No, Neo. I'm trying to tell you that when you are ready, you won't have to."

Fast-forward to the ending when Neo finally internalizes what Morpheus was trying to tell him all along – the matrix is nothing but a computer simulation, where there are no rules, there are no limiting frameworks, there is no need to fight, and there is no death. Empowered by that realization, after a whole lot of slow-motion action sequences, Neo raises his hand, stops the bullets, and learns to fly.

The real trick to a successful reveal is a mix of foreshadowing and looking at the same information from a different angle. If you go back and watch almost any movie where there's a big reveal or an unexpected plot twist, you'll notice that all of the puzzle pieces were right in front of you from the very beginning. Just like stars in a constellation. It's a weird feeling. The entire time, you could sense there was a pattern, but you couldn't quite see it. Or you couldn't see all of it. But then someone comes along – the storyteller, the insight artist – and they reveal one or two stars, one or two clues that you may have overlooked. And with a wave of their hand, they connect the dots in a different way so that everything changes. Everything becomes new. And the world is full of possibilities once again.

CHRIS KOCEK is the founder & CEO of Gallant, a branding agency in Austin, TX dedicated to building brands for a better world. Prior to starting Gallant, Chris worked as a strategic planner at advertising agencies in NYC and Austin, developing nationally recognized campaigns for a number of Fortune 500 brands and highly respected nonprofits, including AARP, Lowe's Home Improvement, Hyatt Hotels, Ace Hardware, John Deere, and The Christopher and Dana Reeve Foundation. In addition to guest lecturing at colleges around the country, Chris is a public speaker whose talks on creativity and innovation have been featured at strategic symposiums as well as TEDx.

For more ideas, observations, and inspiration, go to ChrisKocek.com and sign up for the Light Bulb Newsletter.

Printed in Great Britain
by Amazon

46815854R00099